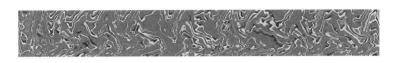

Teaching with Passion, Purpose and Promise

PETER LOEL BOONSHAFT

the Bandstand ltd

Band Instrument Specialists
www.bandstand.ca   mail@bandstand.ca
Fax 780-468-1769   Phone 1-800-661-6352 or 780-465-7264
4824 - 93 Avenue Edmonton AB Canada T6B 2P8

Published by
MEREDITH MUSIC PUBLICATIONS
a division of G.W. Music, Inc.
4899 Lerch Creek Ct., Galesville, MD 20765
http://www.meredithmusic.com

International Standard Book Number: 978-1-57463-153-1
Cataloging-in-Publication Data is on file with the Library of Congress.
Library of Congress Control Number: 2010924165
Printed and bound in U.S.A

Dedication

For my wife, Martha, and my children, Meredith Ann, Peter Loel and Matthew Christopher who have been and always will be my constant source of joy, wonder and beauty in the world. Thank you for your patience and encouragement, your laughter and tears, your spirit and encouragement. I will never be able to express how much you mean to me but I can tell you how much I love you, always.

Acknowledgements

To Dr. Garwood Whaley, Bruce Bush, Reber Clark and Nancy Bittner, thank you for the endlessness of your support, the depth of your wisdom and the abundance of your kindness. Know that how much I appreciate your help is second only to how much I cherish our friendship.

To my family, friends and colleagues, thank you for your encouragement and inspiration.

And, most important, thank you to all of my students who have allowed me the privilege and honor of learning from them. Please know how much I appreciate and cherish each of you.

CONTENTS

PREFACE:
A LITTLE OLD MAN
WHO KNEW

I t was the beginning of September. I was eighteen years old, a freshman in college. There I sat, in an auditorium filled with students, awaiting the start of our opening convocation. Not knowing what to expect, I wondered how it would begin. Would it start with the playing of a fanfare by the brass choir, a rousing anthem by the chorus, or a stirring overture by the symphony orchestra? Would the pipe organ resonate with celebratory strains? Would herald trumpets announce the start of this regal occasion? Would there be pomp and ceremony? Would the faculty process onto the stage wearing long black robes complete with academic hoods? I wondered.

Finally, the lights dimmed, and I realized I was about to find out. After a moment or two, onto the stage shuffled a little old man wearing a tattered old sweater. No robes, no trumpets, no pageantry, no celebration. Just a little old man who looked to be somewhere between ninety and one hundred sixty years of age. A little, unassuming old man who would become one of my greatest teachers. There stood the little old man who would change my life.

"When I was twenty-one," he began, "I knew *everything*. When I was thirty-one, I discovered I could learn a bit more about one or two things. When I was forty-one, I realized there were a *few* things I didn't know. At fifty-one, I recognized there were *many* things I didn't know. At sixty-one, I knew there was a lot I still needed to learn. At seventy-one, I conceded there was more I *didn't* know, than I *did* know. And now I stand here before you, at the age of eighty-one, confident that I don't know *anything*."

I sat there mesmerized as this gentle old man proceeded to talk about the educational journey before us. He spoke about the virtues of hard work, the need to persevere, the importance of patience, the incredible value of every second of time and the splendor of a life dedicated to learning. He spoke passionately, reverently, powerfully. But this wasn't a speech. It wasn't just heartfelt wisdom. This was the evangelical plea of an old man who didn't want any of us — not one person in this auditorium full of young people — to waste a single moment of life. Life, that with each passing day, he found more precious.

Later, I discovered the little old man was the dean emeritus of the college, the elder statesman of the university. The years of studying with him, watching him, and hearing him taught me more than words can say. He taught me as much about what education *could be* as he did about what education *was*. He taught me to learn as much as possible, wherever I could, whenever I could, from whomever I could. He taught me to work hard with all my heart and soul. But mostly, he taught me that someday, if I were lucky, very lucky, I could stand in front of a group of students at the ripe old age of eighty-one and declare the fact that I, too, knew nothing.

I also came to learn that every year would begin this way. Though he, and his age in the story, would grow older with each passing year, the spirit and conviction of his message seemed to grow stronger. Every year, an auditorium full of new young people would sit there, and whether they knew it or not, they would bear witness to the indomitable character, the resolute force that was this little old man. A little old man, with a tattered old sweater, who changed my life by teaching me what he *didn't know*, as much as he did with what he *did know*. A little old man who embodied the words of the great Michelangelo, who at the age of eighty-seven said, "Ancora imparo," simply, "Still I am learning."

It is with that spirit, and the belief that those who think they have all the answers don't really know the questions, that this book was written. There are no answers here, no right or better way to do anything. What follows is simply food for thought, ideas to mull over. Some ideas you will recognize as *what you do* and *who you are* every day. Some you will recognize as "old friends" you have not thought about for a while which you may decide to revisit. Some may be new and worth consideration, while others may cause us to disagree strongly.

And do you know what? All of those possibilities are wonderful. For what could be better than for each of us to confirm our thoughts, challenge our beliefs and strengthen our resolve? Sometimes, trying new ideas or thinking new thoughts can be more liberating than enlightening, more creatively thought-provoking than instructional. Especially if we always remember that the *right way* isn't always the opposite of the *wrong way*.

All any of us can do is spend our lives asking questions, searching for answers, trying new ideas, testing, seeking, looking, exploring, aspiring for better. Better for ourselves, our students, our communities and our world. A world every teacher changes one student at a time. And in so doing, we honor those who have entrusted themselves to us, just as we entrusted ourselves to those who taught us.

I guess it all boils down to shoulders. Yes, you read correctly, *shoulders*. More precisely, being *appreciative* of shoulders. For teachers — we whose purpose it is to take the knowledge of the past, add to it, then pass it on to the next generation to do the same — no words could be more perfect than those of Sir Isaac Newton: "If I have seen farther, it is by standing upon the shoulders of giants." I am so appreciative of the giants in my life — my family, friends, colleagues, teachers and students — who have allowed me to see by my standing upon their wise and talented shoulders. They have taught me and will always continue to teach me.

In fact, this book is a collection of that which I have learned from my teachers and students. It also contains many quotes from people far more learned than I will ever be. Every effort has been made to correctly attribute those thoughts; however, where the author is believed to be unknown, no ascription has been made.

I also want to thank *you* for reading these pages, and for sharing with me the journey that is teaching and learning. Words do not exist that express my appreciation for your kindness and support. My thanks for all you do as teachers, mentors and beacons is matched only by my awe at your commitment, dedication and talents. On behalf of every student whose life you touch, thank you. Thank you for what you do and who you are, but, even more, for that which you help your students to learn and for whom you help them to become. No promise could be more important than that. No passion could be greater than that. No journey could be more joyous. And rich are the people who spend their lives so nobly, with such purpose.

"Purpose." What an amazing word. A word I chose as part of the title of this book because of its various and wonderful meanings, every aspect of which we — as teachers — personify. For indeed, we teach with the purpose of perseverance, determination and drive; the purpose that is our intent, end and goal; and the purpose that is our reason, rationale and principle. But what *is* our purpose? What is the *purpose* of teaching?

Each of us answers those questions in our own way every time we stand before a room full of students, every time we look into their eyes, every time we encourage them to touch the stars, every time we help them reveal their souls, every time we get them to cry or laugh, every time we help them learn, every time we make them realize the wonder and greatness that is them.

Amazing, isn't it? All that from a person who cares more than others can conceive. We call them teachers: those people who selflessly dedicate their lives to a profoundly fantastic journey. May the journey of your teaching be as magnificent and full of wonder as those students with whom you share it. ▧

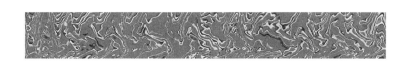

PROMISE

It had been one of those weeks. Thanks to some very poor planning on my part I had crossed the country from coast to coast six times in eight days, including two red-eye flights through the night. Don't ask why. Let's just say that my brain still thinks I'm twenty-five though my body knows the truth of the matter. If that wasn't bad enough, severe winter weather caused delay upon delay upon delay. After over a week of this I arrived home in New York late one evening run ragged, left with raw nerves, little patience, a faint memory of what sleep felt like and the desire to curl up in a corner somewhere and hide from the world. But I couldn't.

That's right, you guessed it: the next morning I had to be at the airport by 4:45 for yet another flight to another state on the West Coast. So after unpacking and repacking my suitcase, an extravagant four hours of sleep and a leisurely breakfast of black coffee on the run, I was off to catch my flight. It was pitch black outside, well below freezing, with snow everywhere. Walking down the driveway from my house I slipped and fell on the ice. Now wet, cold and sore, I drove to the airport, seething. I was at wit's end, dreading a day that had barely started.

I boarded the airplane and just sat there as waves of feeling frazzled, hungry, exhausted, drained and angry surged through me. I was anything but hopeful, everything but positive. The darkness outside was a perfect match for my mood. Well, as we taxied away from the ramp, I started doing paperwork so I could add some worry about how far behind I was to my gloominess. As we flew south to avoid yet another storm, something caught my eye outside the window.

It was a tiny glimmer of light. It almost looked like a spark way off in the distance and as I continued to stare at it the little shard of brightness grew larger and larger filling the darkness with radiance. I couldn't take my eyes off it. It was captivating. It was mesmerizing. It was overwhelming. It was breathtaking. It was a sunrise. Now I've watched sunrises before, glancing occasionally at that beautiful sight, but this was different. On that day I didn't just watch a *sunrise*, I watched the *sun rise*. I watched as it filled emptiness with brilliance and shattered uncertainty with clarity. Its luster brought optimism. Its glow signaled hope. It was the light of promise.

As I watched, all the ills I carried with me onto that airplane slipped away, my spirit was uplifted, my mood transformed. I was charged with excitement about the trip I had dreaded little more than an hour before. My thoughts filled with the possibilities of what was ahead of me, the enjoyment around the corner and the importance of every moment I get to teach young people. I smiled with enthusiasm as that light revealed what really mattered. With that sunrise I realized what I guess I always knew — what each of us always knew — that along with teaching with passion and teaching with purpose, it is our teaching with promise that may make all the difference in the lives of our students.

The promise of teaching found in every new day, in what the future holds, in the untapped potential we help every child realize. The promise we affirm as teachers to make a difference, to help students discover the people they are and the people they can become. The promise of knowledge, skills, creativity and caring. The promise of hope, enthusiasm, optimism and resolve. The promise of high expectations, astonishing dedication, unending commitment, sincere concern and heartfelt counsel. Quite simply, the promise of a teacher.

Teacher, instructor, mentor — by whatever name you call them — those who have devoted themselves to bettering the world one person at a time. Those who excite minds, deepen hearts, touch souls and change lives. Those whose impact is greater than any moment in time, whose reach is farther than any place, whose destiny is more profound than any estimation, whose promise is more valuable than any fortune.

May you realize your gifts and cherish your importance. May you seek out and find those everyday moments of joy and happiness. May you cherish every smile, every tear and every laugh. May you reflect upon all you do for your students, that which may be found in a book or sheet of paper and that which is so much greater.

With each new day, each new sunrise, we have the opportunity to imagine what can be and make it happen. For each of us the excitement of every new beginning is the promise of what lies ahead, what can be, what the future holds. Much like an artist looks at a blank canvas and sees the beauty that will soon be created, we as teachers see the child that can be, a treasure waiting to be discovered, ever mindful that what we *see* depends on what we *look* for. Never lose sight of that incredible responsibility or the richness of that calling.

But maybe when all is said and done, the best way to really describe the promise of teaching is to borrow a sentiment from the inimitable Marx Brothers, with the query: Did you know that there is a million bucks hidden in the house next door? The reply: But there is no house next door. Undaunted, the response: No? Then let's go build one.

Funny as it may be, isn't that just what you do every day? You see the fortune all children are as you build the house they will find themselves in. And that, my friends, is the passion, purpose and promise of teaching. ▧

"Education is Fundamentally an Imaginative Act of Hope"

O f all the negative feelings we humans are capable of, what do you think is the worst? Hate? Anxiety? Fear? I believe the worst is *frustration*. I think it is the root cause of so many destructive emotions, especially for teachers. Frustration causes anxiety, burnout, apathy, anger and so many other roadblocks. At the very least it sidetracks each of us from being the teacher we want to be.

But let's face it, what we do is often frustrating. I certainly don't need to list all the sources of frustration we teachers face day in and day out. However, I think the one that is *most* worrisome to me is the frustration of where our students are now *versus* where we want them to be. And the weaker we perceive them to be, the worse that frustration seems. Knowing what it will take to move them to that goal can be daunting.

Staying positive and hopeful in the face of educational hurdles is difficult, but doing so when faced with extraordinary challenges can sometimes put us over the edge. What follows are a few thoughts I have used as guides through those sometimes murky and confusing times.

Be Hopeful

No matter the cause of our frustration, we must remember those words of William Purkey and John Novak which title this chapter: "Education is fundamentally an imaginative act of hope." That really sums up everything I believe. It is the alpha and the omega of education. We're just a bunch of optimists, or we wouldn't be in this profession. Put simply, we just can't be frustrated with how badly our students perform or how little they know.

See Greatness

We can't lose sight of the fact that our job is to see the greatness in our students, not just in their ability, but in them as people. Sure, it's easy to see faults and shortcomings, but as their teachers, we must look deeper into their eyes and see the greatness that lies inside. Sometimes I think students don't show their greatness because no one has ever believed it was there.

Presume Excellence

Self-fulfilling prophecies work for each of us as people, but I think they work just as powerfully for us as teachers. If we presume a student or group of students will struggle to achieve, they *will* struggle to achieve. If we think they will end up being some of our weakest students, they will. However, if we assume our students will be high achievers and expect they will excel, more than likely, they will. I know this sounds like so much psychobabble, but I believe it more than I can express. They *will* become what we think they will become. They will become the vision, however good or bad, of what we see in them.

In Reverse

Sometimes the best way to get students to where we want them to be is to *envision them there*. Picture the goal point. Then plot backwards from there, step by step, to where they are now. Working from "finish" to "start" can sometimes be exhilarating and empowering.

Believe in Them

They must be convinced that *you are convinced* they will achieve the goal. Sometimes it is less about their believing they can, and more about their believing *we believe* they can! Students can't, unless we help them believe they can.

Stepping Stones

Every new challenge our students face along their paths can be seen as a stepping stone *or* as a stumbling block; the former serving to lift them up, the latter to knock them down. We have to convince them those "bars" we keep raising are steps to their success rather than obstacles in their path.

Facilitated Expectations

When we come to class with an expectation, a goal, do we also come with a procedure to get there? In other words, do we facilitate accomplishing that goal with a detailed lesson plan to make it happen? If students are given a planned, prioritized procedure to get there, they *can* do it. Expectations alone are lofty ambitions; facilitated expectations are a staircase to success.

Take a Giant Step Backwards

When students sense they are doing poorly, they can become like mules: very hard to move forward, very willing to stay put. If we start them with material "easy" enough that they succeed, in short order, they start to become like the little engine that could: thinking they can. It's so easy for our students to "throw in the towel" when *they think* they are already defeated. However, it is also easy for them to become motivated by early success.

Think of it like dieting. Sadly, I have had more than my fair share of dieting, so I can speak as an expert. Ask anyone who has dieted; it's easy to stay motivated in the first few days because the pounds fall off with relative ease. Success breeds success, so we stay on track with enthusiasm. The problem comes after a few days, when the plateaus start and frustration sets in. Perceived frustration breeds a feeling the goal cannot be achieved, which makes it very, very easy to give up. Then it's donut shop here I come!

Even if that means we start the year with material or activities far easier than desired, so be it, if it allows our students to sense the joy of excellence. Sometimes a big step backwards can make possible many steps forward.

Vitamins: The Right Prescription

I take vitamins every day. I have for years. I am earnest about it. But why? Why do I take them? I don't know if they are doing anything for me. I have never seen any immediate results or specific effects from them, the way I have from aspirin or antibiotics. So why take them? Well I hope that by taking them every day, they will build up in my body and keep me healthy. At some point they may keep me from getting some awful disease. But I really don't know. Again, it all comes down to hope. I am willing to stick with it, confident in the knowledge they are the right prescription — a prescription that will pay off in the future.

Sometimes the results of what we teach are seen in an instant, but often what we teach becomes the "vitamins" of education. Can we always know when we will see the results of our work? No. Will the benefits of what we teach always be seen? Maybe not. But good teaching, like vitamins, may determine a child's educational future more than we think.

Which Frog?

Sometimes the weakest starters end up being the best finishers. And the truth is we don't really know which "frog," with the "kiss" of great teaching, will become a "prince." Even those students who start as "frog" learners can become "prince" successes, if we measure success by how much they

It is said that with great honor comes great responsibility, and with the honor of being a teacher comes the responsibility of three little words in the Latin phrase, "in loco parentis," or "in the place of the parent." What could be more weighty a pledge than to promise to act in the best interest of every student? What could be more important an obligation than to honor the confidence of every parent? More profound responsibilities I cannot imagine.

Every day, parents give us their most treasured gifts — their children — confident we will guard their safety, nourish their souls, stimulate their minds and inspire their imaginations. It is that sacred trust we must honor. It is that sacred trust which explains why teaching is a calling, not just a career. It is that sacred trust that makes clear why we don't need to make a change in the world to make a difference in the world.

The promise of the future, the promise of our students, the promise of our world depends upon those who teach. For we are the guardians of *those we teach* as much as *what we teach*. Three *little* words indeed. ▪

"YES, IF..."

I spend a lot of time in airplanes. My travels have me up in the sky far more than any sane person should be. But even with all that time in the air, and despite the fact that I have a private pilot's license and learned all the theory behind *how it works*, not a flight goes by on one of those jumbo jets where I don't marvel at the fact that it does. How can a couple of comparatively small engines lift, let alone keep, ninety collective tons of metal, fiberglass, plastic — and those little bags of pretzels or peanuts — soaring in the sky? Really now, how can that be?

More important, why would anyone propose we do it, let alone think it possible in the first place? I'm telling you, if Wilbur and Orville Wright had come to me back in the days when they were trying to get manned flight "off the ground" I would have given them fifty reasons why it couldn't have worked. Less than a century later, even though modest-sized jet airplanes filled the skies, designers wanted to create airplanes so large they could only be described as flying fortresses weighing well over three-quarters of a million pounds, each capable of carrying half a dozen symphony orchestras at a time with room for their choruses to boot. And you know what? They did it. How? How can that much weight lift from the earth and traverse the heavens with abandon? Far more important than the *how* of it working is the *how* of those who willed it to happen. How did they make the unfathomable possible? In my mind, the answers to each of those questions are intimately related. Let me explain.

Let's pretend I was back with Wilbur and Orville when they decided they wanted to be birds, or at least fly like them. There we are sitting around their bicycle shop in Dayton, Ohio when Orville says, "So, Peter, we're thinking of building a flying machine that can take a man soaring through the skies. Do you think it can work?"

My immediate answer would have been, "*No, because* it will never be sturdy enough to withstand those stresses, falling apart before it ever leaves the ground. *No, because* even if it didn't fall apart, you would have no control of the airplane rolling left or right and it would crash. *No, because* even if you could control the banking of the airplane left and right you still couldn't control the pitch of the nose moving up or down. *No, because* even if that didn't happen you would never get enough sustained lift to fight the power of gravity so you would plummet back to earth. *No, because* even if you solved that you could never stop the yaw of the airplane and it would go into an uncontrollable slip. *No, because* even if that weren't the result there is no design for an airplane propeller that works, and finally *no, because* an engine powerful enough to provide the necessary speed for sustained flight would be far too heavy to allow the airplane to get off the ground. So no, it can never work!"

There you have it, the pursuit of manned flight ended

in one brief conversation. Without a doubt, if I were there that day and the Wright brothers listened to me, we would still be dreaming of flight, convinced man would never fly. Why? Because I was an *inhibitor*, serving to convince those visionary brothers that failure was not just possible, it was assured. Using the language of an inhibitor, starting every sentence with "No, because," I succeeded in dooming dreams-of-what-had-never-been-achieved to the realm of the impossible. The unlikely became the unattainable, the hopeful became the hopeless, the promising became the unrealistic.

I would have surely destroyed the spirits of even the most optimistic inventor. Here, as is often the case, *defending why something is not possible is far easier than figuring out how to make that very same thing possible.*

What was so different during those historic days *without me* there to inhibit the Wright brothers? Well the true greatness of Wilbur and Orville rested in their perseverance and indomitable spirit, but even more important was their ability to *enable* their efforts. They were far less interested in why manned flight had not been achieved and far more interested in what manned flight could be.

My guess is the conversation between those bold visionaries probably went something like this: "So, Orville, let's talk about our dream of building a flying machine that can take a man soaring through the skies. Do you think it can work?" To which Wilbur replied, "*Yes, if* we figure out a way to build it sturdy enough to withstand the stresses of takeoff so it doesn't fall apart before it ever leaves the ground. *Yes, if* we invent a way to control the airplane rolling left or right so it won't crash after liftoff. *Yes, if* we come up with a way to control the pitch of the airplane making it possible to aim the nose up and down. *Yes, if* we develop a way to create enough lift to fight the power of gravity so we won't plummet back to earth once we are airborne. *Yes, if* we devise a way to stop the sideways yaw movement of the airplane's tail so we prevent an uncontrollable slip. *Yes, if* we design a propeller which effectively pulls the aircraft forward, and finally *yes, if* we build an engine powerful enough to provide the necessary speed for takeoff and sustained flight yet light enough to allow the airplane to get off the ground. So yes, it can absolutely work!"

What really was the difference? Was it just a matter of semantics? I don't think so. In the words of Harrison Price, a significant figure in making the dreams of Walt Disney a reality, "'Yes, if…' is the language of an enabler." Those words, *that language*, pointing "to what needed to be done to make the possible plausible." Whereas, "No, because…" inhibits progress, "Yes, if…" paves the way for it.

As Napoleon Hill so clearly put it, "Whatever the mind of man can conceive and believe, it can achieve." The language of an enabler helps people to conceive and believe so they *can* achieve by simply describing what must be done next. The language of an inhibitor convinces people the goal is impossible because the path to it is catastrophically overwhelming. To the inhibitor, defeat is not only possible, it is a foregone conclusion, warranting no further effort or thought. To the enabler, success is not only possible with the steps toward it clearly in focus, it is assured. So the Wright brothers, enablers both, set out to make their dream come true by solving one concern at a time, secure — at the core — of the outcome.

With each confident "yes, if" of their journey, they answered the question or solved the problem, with that spirit inspiring their actions toward refuting the belief that it could not be done. By simply working from their success in bicycle design, and much trial and error, they figured out better methods to make an airplane's construction sturdier.

One day, while twisting a long thin box in his hands, Wilbur came up with the idea to use a series of cables to control the raising or lowering of each wing with a system he called "wing-warping." This warping or twisting of the wings allowed the airplane to safely bank to the left or right, controlling the rolling movement of the plane.

Next they discovered that by using a movable horizontal surface called an elevator, they could control the pitch of their craft, making it nose up or down as desired.

To find a way to create and sustain enough lift to fight the power of gravity, the brothers tested over two hundred wing shapes, or airfoils, in a wind tunnel until they found the one which produced the most lift.

To solve the problem of the airplane sliding or skidding sideways, the yaw motion which made it difficult to control the craft in a turn, a movable rudder with its own controls replaced the fixed tail. This provided the ability to point the nose of the airplane left or right, preventing uncontrollable slips or skids while warping the wings.

Realizing that an airplane's propeller had to function like a rotating wing, they designed the first effective airplane propeller, able to pull the aircraft forward with great power.

Unable to find an engine powerful enough to provide the necessary speed for takeoff and to keep the airplane aloft once airborne—also light enough to allow the airplane to get off the ground — Wilbur and Orville decided to design and build their own lightweight yet robust one.

Basically, the Wright brothers willed this dream to happen by inventing each technology or system needed to solve each successive step toward their goal. Their beginning mindset provided no preconceived barriers to stop progress before it happened; rather it simply identified what needed to be accomplished for each step as they moved closer to accomplishing what they set out to do.

Can I prove that either Wilbur or Orville Wright ever once uttered the two words — "Yes, if" — as they changed the course of history? No. Though I am sure the spirit of that expression led them to accomplish what others gave up on, others who started with a litany of phrases that began with "No, because."

But I am certain that for a child who is lacking the courage of Wilbur and Orville, less driven or motivated, more frightened or insecure, the words they hear from us, the attitude we convey, the steps for success versus reasons for failure matter greatly. In the classroom, couldn't we agree that even the most dedicated student would just plain "give up" if confronted with an inhibitor, irrespective of how well-intentioned that teacher may be? Conversely, how could that same student help but be caught up in the groundswell of confidence and encouraging plan of action set out by the enabling teacher?

Where inhibitors give reasons why something can't be done, enablers give reasons why it will be done. As teachers we decide whether a student will think "I would if I could, but *I can't* so *I won't*," or "I would if I could, and *I can* so *I will*." They are not just words, they are prophecies.

Tennessee Williams affirmed, "The future is called 'perhaps,' which is the only possible thing to call the future. And the important thing is not to allow that to scare you." As teachers we often control whether the future scares our students into giving up before they even start or inspires them to continue since their success is assured. As Antoine de Saint-Exupéry so eloquently wrote, "When it comes to the future, our task is not to foresee it, but rather to enable it to happen."

We decide whether our students will believe the words of Bernard Edmonds: "To dream anything that you want to dream. That is the beauty of the human mind. To do anything that you want to do. That is the strength of the human will. To trust yourself to test your limits. That is the courage to succeed." We decide whether our students succeed because they *didn't know they couldn't*. We decide whether our students embrace the spirit of Robert Louis Stevenson's brilliant sentiment: "To be what we are, and to become what we are capable of becoming, is the only end of life."

For our students, quite simply, our thinking and acting like enablers may not change *the* world, but it can change *their* world. Can we really do that? *Yes, if…*

JAKE, JOHNNY AND A LESSON WELL LEARNED

One of my first teaching experiences was offering beginning band and instrumental lessons in a very small elementary school. More specifically, in the *boiler room* of a very small elementary school. Now I know many of you may have taught in a boiler room, but my boiler was bigger than your boiler. For you see in this tiny school was a furnace slightly larger than the one needed to heat the surface of the sun. It was enormous, slightly older than Moses, and when it kicked on shook the room while making noises similar to a revving 747 aircraft on takeoff. But the best part was when it started up and blew black soot from a small vent on its side.

Small group lessons were a sight to behold: a gaggle of fourth graders working on deep-breathing exercises as a cloud of smoke billowed past them. I feared we would all finish the year with black lung disease. And if the soot wasn't bad enough I could barely hear them make a sound over the rumble of what seemed like centuries-old grinding steel from this boiler first installed in that school when George Washington was in beginning band. It was horrible in ways I simply can't describe.

Well this went on for a few weeks until I just couldn't take it anymore. It had to stop. So I went up to the principal's office, knocked on her door and asked if we could speak. She invited me in, wondering what was on my mind. I proceeded to tell her that I could not continue to teach in the boiler room, that it was an impossible situation and that I had to be moved. After I vented for a few minutes, she put her hand up in the air like a stop sign and interrupted me. "Peter," she said, "great teachers can teach anywhere. So go back to your boiler room and be a great teacher." Instantly I was defused, disarmed, dejected and depressed. Crestfallen, I scuffed back to my room unable to muster another word, not smart enough to find a retort to rebut those paralyzing words. What else could I do but return to my lessons, complete with clouds of soot and accompaniments of rumbling machinery.

As the days went on I got angrier and more disillusioned. I finally decided I could take it no longer. One of us—the boiler or me—had to go. So I decided I would march into the principal's office and threaten to quit, before I realized she could go ahead and take me up on the offer! Then it hit me. I had what might just be a solution.

I made my way back to the principal's office, knocked on her door and told her I had a problem. She looked straight into my eyes and said, "Not that boiler room thing again, I thought we settled that." "No," I replied, "the problem is me." Looking puzzled, she asked what I meant. "I can't do it," I said. Looking even more puzzled, she queried, "Do what?" I went on to answer, "I have this one lesson group of clarinet students I can't reach. I can't connect with them and I just don't know what to do. I need help." Now looking more concerned than baffled, she immediately offered to help. "When's the next time you'll see them?" she inquired. "Tomorrow morning at nine o'clock," I replied with a pensive voice. "Then I'll be there," she said, "and we'll see what's wrong." My head hanging low, my face showing great concern, I thanked her and walked out of the office.

Once out of sight, I zoomed to the custodian's office to find Jake, our head custodian. As luck would have it I walked into the room and there he was. "Jake," I said with a respectful air of seriousness, "I need a favor." Always willing to help in any way, he said, "What do you need?" I replied, "Jake, I need the furnace to kick on at exactly 9:02 tomorrow morning. Not 9:01 or 9:03, but 9:02 on the dot." His obvious answer was, "Why?" "Better you don't know," I said with a knowing grin, "but can you do it?" He said, "Well yes, but I'm gonna need some help." "Help?" I said, "to turn on a switch?" He said, "Yep, I'm gonna need help from Johnny." Thinking for a moment, knowing we had no custodian by that name, I said, "Johnny? Johnny who?" He said, "Johnny Walker." "The booze?" I replied. He said, "Well, you might call it that." He then went on to say, "If Johnny gets here about 8:30 or so, I bet that boiler would kick on about 9:02."

So I ran to the closest liquor store and bought the biggest bottle of Johnny Walker I could afford, put a note on it that read "9:02 on the dot," and placed it judiciously on Jake's desk in the custodian's office. I then bolted to my room — the boiler room, that is — and proceeded to remove every chair but the eight I needed for the clarinet lesson (and the one for the principal, of course).

The next morning I made sure the boiler room was tidy and neat, or as tidy and neat as a boiler room can be, and checked that the chair count was just right. At about 8:50 my clarinetists arrived and took their seats, readying themselves to play. As I chatted with my students I heard a rap on the open door. Looking up, I welcomed the principal and showed her to her waiting chair which, coincidence of coincidences, happened to be right next to the vent alongside the furnace.

I then began my lesson with some introductory remarks before starting a series of warm-up exercises. Seemingly settled and comfortable, my smiling principal looked around, no doubt checking the orderliness of my room. All was fine; students, teacher and principal were doing well.

Staring at the clock like a hawk, I launched into a few deep-breathing exercises at 9:01, working at getting my charges to suck in more and more air. With each passing exercise — and second on the clock — I watched as the sweep-second hand moved ever closer to the twelve. With a few seconds to spare I asked the kids to draw in as much air as they could.

Just then, I swear to you, like a bad "B movie" in slow motion, I watched the sweep-second hand hit 9:02. At that moment my students prepared to take the deepest breaths of their lives as the furnace started up with a thunderous rumble, spewing black soot from its vent. Jake came through. As my young clarinetists sucked in black smoke and began coughing, the principal jumped from her chair, waved her hand to clear the cloud of soot and began yelling,

"What *is* that!" With a calm look of nonplussed bewilderment I replied, "What is *what*?" "That noise and all that smoke," she shouted, "what *is* that?" "The boiler," I said with complete composure. "Peter," she authoritatively replied, "this is a totally unsuitable teaching environment. You've got to be moved." "Can you do that?" I asked with a sense of awe. "I can do *anything*," she barked, "I am the principal."

But be careful what you wish for. The next morning I was teaching in the lobby of the gymnasium! No problem teaching breathing; now my biggest challenge was getting kids to play with a steady pulse as they heard fifty basketballs, each dribbling at a different tempo. But I was out of the boiler room and that was all that mattered.

The whole thing is almost incomprehensible: that a teacher — any teacher — would have to teach in a boiler room; that a bottle of spirits could make a furnace come to life; that a principal wouldn't see through such an obvious plan; that a teacher would have to teach in the lobby of a gymnasium; that teaching in that lobby could be seen as a step up to the finest of facilities; or that a young music teacher would learn one of the most valuable lessons of his life.

For on that day my friend Jake and his friend Johnny taught me a lesson that has served me well for all these years. I most vividly learned that tact, diplomacy and finesse can get just about anything accomplished, while demands, tantrums and threats almost never do. Now I would be lying if I didn't tell you that deep inside, my knee-jerk reaction is still to "threaten to quit" or some other such manner of throwing a fit, but when I stop and think — *really* think — I always remember Jake, Johnny and that lesson well learned.

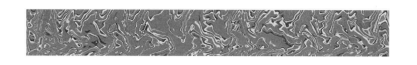

BROCCOLI

I'm guessing you are trying to figure out what broccoli — yes, that green bulbous vegetable — could possibly have to do with education or being a better teacher. Well, I believe a lot. Let me try to explain.

As teachers, when we are presented with ideas, we can react many different ways, though generally they fall into three broad categories.

The first reaction is agreement: the technique is exactly what you do, we basically agree. We could start a club and start printing t-shirts. The second reaction brings somewhat less agreement, but agreement nonetheless. It may be you did it that way in the past but forgot about it, or you do something very similar, or you would be willing to try it to see if you like it, or you feel aspects of the approach could be blended with your current method. You may not want to join the club but you would wear the t-shirt if it were free.

The third reaction is contempt. As the words describing the technique pass from my lips you are utterly appalled, aghast at what I'm espousing, downright angered by the very thought of what I am suggesting. You not only don't currently do it that way, or anything like that way, but the very idea makes you cringe. You wouldn't use the t-shirt as a dust rag.

Though the first reaction is okay and the second is fine, my favorite is the third. Why, you ask? Well it is always nice to find people who agree on a topic. It helps one confirm the validity and soundness of the idea. But having people strongly disagree means they are as fervent in their beliefs as I am in mine. Disagreements like that make for continued growth and development, challenging each of us to re-evaluate what we think. Even if we end up with the same opinion, the process of testing our viewpoint is so very beneficial.

Without question, the third reaction is wonderful, but only if people do not come to their adamant belief the way my son came to his opinion about broccoli.

You see, years ago, when my son Peter was the ripe old age of three or four, our family was sitting around the kitchen table for dinner. It was a dinner I will never forget. Holding a large bowl of steamed broccoli, I said, "Peter, would you like some broccoli?" He replied, "No." I asked why. He quite firmly declared, "I hate broccoli." So I said, "You hate broccoli, but have you ever tried it?" To that he incredulously said, "Dad, why would I ever try something that I hate?" Dumbfounded, I looked at my wife and said, "How do you argue with that logic?" Why indeed would anyone try something they hate?

Now you're still wondering what this can possibly have to do with teaching. Well many of us come to our resolute opinions about ideas, techniques or materials the same way my son arrived at his attitude about broccoli. We learned a way of doing something in college, taught to us by someone we respected, so we have continued to use it to this day, defending it in our minds as the best way. Sometimes it becomes so crystallized in our minds that we don't challenge it, seek to modify or improve it, or look for better ways. We are almost petrified in place, seemingly fearing lightning bolts from heaven if we dare stray from *that* way.

Certainly those ideas from long ago may be the best way, leaving you completely justified in your reaction. But sometimes I fear we take them as the best way only because someone once told us they were. My hope is that we challenge any belief, verify any information, test any approach and experiment with new paths to any goal. New ideas *can* be better and we must be open to trying them. We may find something we like better and choose to adopt it, not because it is new, but because we deem it better. Likewise, some time-tested approaches may be the best way, not because they are old, but because they work well.

Any idea worth its salt should be able to withstand challenge. Often, challenging tenets we hold dear can be difficult but challenge them we must. We owe it to our students, our profession and ourselves to seek the best approaches to our goals, defending them because we have reason, real reason, to do so. Remember, if people hadn't challenged what they had been taught, the medical profession would still be teaching doctors to bleed patients with leeches.

So the next time you are presented with a new way of doing something, however peculiar it may seem, remember my son and his broccoli; more important, remember how growth and progress more often than not come from the simple quest to find a better way. If nothing else, what a wonderful lesson that is for our students to learn from our example. Quite simply, when they see us try new or different ways, test assumptions or challenge our usual ways, they learn that doing so is healthy and constructive. That is a lesson that will serve them well, a lesson far more important than simply trying broccoli. ▪

AND THERE SAT FRANKLIN

I grew up in a wonderful community just outside of Philadelphia. Our home was filled with a great deal of love,
thanks in no small measure to a very large dog and three
cats. The veterinarian who cared for our four-legged family
members was a remarkably warm-hearted doctor known
for being a great veterinarian. He was also renowned for
having toilet-trained his own family's cats. That's right, you
read correctly, toilet-trained his cats. And having grown up
my whole childhood hearing about his (or was it his cats')
remarkable feat, I always wanted to have a toilet-trained cat
myself.

Now I told you that story so I could tell you this story.
Many, many years later when I was living in my first apartment, I got a cat; his name was Franklin. One weekend my
parents came to visit for a few days. After showing them
around the apartment, I sat down with my dad in the living
room to chat while my mom excused herself to go to the
bathroom. The next thing I heard was my mom shriek-
ing at the top of her lungs in exasperated bafflement and

quasi-disgust as she walked in on Franklin as he was, well, let's just say using the toilet. That's right, Franklin my toilet-trained cat.

I ran to the bathroom and there was Mom pointing at the cat while he was doing his business. He looked at her as if to say, "Hey lady, can I have a little privacy here?" To say the least, Mom was shocked. To me it was normal. I was used to seeing my furry friend sitting on the toilet reading a good book (okay, I made the book part up). I became dulled to how odd it was. It became usual and normal to me.

Now I told you that story so I could tell you this story. A few years back I was invited to speak in a town that was several hours' drive from the closest airport. After landing there I met my host, we jumped into his car and started our journey. Midway through our drive I began to smell something odd. Odd then grew to bad, bad grew to disgusting, disgusting grew to nauseating and nauseating grew to repulsive. Finally, in amazement at this stench, I asked my host what I was smelling. Completely unaffected, he nonchalantly replied, "Oh, that's the local paper mill."

I don't know if you've ever been near a paper mill, but let me tell you, they emit an odor that would offend a gaggle (okay, it's really a "wake") of buzzards feasting at the city garbage dump. It is a smell like no other. So there I was, gasping for breath, my eyes watering, my throat tightening, while he sat totally oblivious to the hideous stench. Then he said, "I guess when you're around it as much as I am, you don't even smell it anymore." How true. How incredibly true. He grew comfortable with something even as unpleasant as that smell. It simply became normal to him.

Now I told you that story so I could tell you this story.

Last evening I attended a high school band concert. As the students walked onto the stage they looked polished and professional. Their posture was wonderful and they glowed with confidence. All of us in the audience were convinced a stupendous performance was in store. The conductor then began the first piece on the program and I'm guessing the band probably played reasonably well. Why am I guessing at how well they played, when I was sitting right in front of them, you ask? Because it was almost impossible to hear anything other than the bass drum being played at a volume that could only be described as explosively loud. I'm telling you sparks were coming off that bass drum beater.

From the first downbeat right through to the final note, I was convinced the bass drummer's part said, "Play so loudly that the ears of every member of the audience bleed." It was utterly astounding. I watched and listened in disbelief as the young man playing the bass drum beat the daylights out of the instrument with unbridled power. How could that have happened? How could that teacher's senses have become so dulled to that sound? How could he not have noticed it? Easily, if we are not careful and vigilant, we can become used to just about anything.

So why did I tell you that story? To remind us that we are all susceptible to things becoming *usual* enough that we expect them, accept them and grow oblivious to them. Maybe it's the loud rumbling of a radiator in our class-room which makes hearing the teacher difficult, or the glare of sunlight from a window which makes seeing the board impossible, or the sights from outside the classroom windows which cause distractions, or the mind-numbing tediousness of certain activities which become routine to students, or a teacher's mannerisms that make students feel ill at ease. True, most things won't be as odd as the sight of a cat on the toilet, as offensive as the smell of a paper mill or as thunderously blaring as a rampant bass drummer, but they can be distracting, detrimental or damaging nonetheless. And if they *creep into* our perception of normal, they can easily become ignored.

Put simply, our perception — if changed gradually enough or for long enough periods of time — can be altered without our being aware of it, allowing us to become used to just about anything. How else could that conductor have become oblivious to his bass drummer's playing, my host become unaware of the paper mill's repulsive odor, or I grow so used to seeing my cat on a toilet as to be unfazed?

Though those stories are unquestionably extreme examples, they do remind us to be ever vigilant, ultra prepared, keenly aware, highly focused and intensely observant. We are all susceptible to that same kind of numbing of our senses if we don't guard against it and take steps to prevent it.

We all need to step back from the situation to look and listen for things that have become normal to us. We know simply recording our classes can be amazingly insightful. Enlisting the help of other teachers in your school and district, or getting local college instructors and retired educators to sit in on classes, can give you fresh sets of eyes and ears of those who can objectively critique the session without the unconscious unawareness of that to which you have grown accustomed. Changing the setup of our classrooms or having the students sit in odd configurations can offer us different vantage points and perspectives with just enough difference to shake up our perception of normal, refreshing our eyes, ears and minds.

Quite simply, to fend off the problem of getting used to things in our classrooms, mix equal parts awareness, concern, concentration, observation and attentiveness. Stir in a fair amount of objectivity and serve it in the clear glass of keen perception, with a sprig of utter delight.

Like seeing something as unusual as a cat using the toilet, or smelling an odor offensive enough to curl hair, or hearing a student beating the daylights out of a bass drum, if we see, smell or hear anything often enough, unless we stay on guard, it can become normal to us, rendering us completely and absolutely oblivious to it.

By the way, in case you ever come visit my home, let me warn you about our cat Janet, the one who knows how to turn on the water spigot when she wants a drink. But that's a story for another day. ▧

SHARE THE GOAL

"So much to teach — so little time." For teachers, could truer words be written? *How much* we must teach to help our students reach the goals we set, and *how well* we must teach it, demand such incredible patience, pacing, planning and perseverance. A casualty, however, of this race against the clock is often one of the most important determining factors of reaching those very goals. Quite simply it's the question of *who* knows what the goal is.

When speaking about this topic to a room full of teachers, I use a simple demonstration to make my point. I stand in front of them, pause in silence, then at the top of my lungs scream the word, "Run!" That's right, in the middle of a crowded room I scream the word "run" with all the power and vehemence I can muster. No matter how many times I do this, no matter where I am, the response never ceases to amaze me. No one moves. No one. In fact my comment to those in attendance is always the same: "Do you realize that not one of you even bothered to uncross your legs, let alone got up and ran?"

Then I try it again with one slight difference. This time I stand in front of them, pause in silence, then proceed to calmly say, "Ladies and gentleman, this auditorium is on fire. You need to *run* to the nearest exit and get outside immediately." Were it not for the fact they knew I was making a point rather than an announcement, you could bet their collective fannies would be out that door before you could blink. Why? Because this time I shared the goal with them so they knew the reason why they should run, saw the value in running and understood the purpose of my asking them to run. Armed with that information they knew why they were running as well as to where they were running.

How many of us can think back to countless hours of homework, class lectures, activities and assignments *our* teachers asked us to do with our never knowing why? Surely the teacher knew why he or she was asking us to do whatever it was, but we didn't. Not knowing why we were doing it, why it was important or why it was worthwhile, we had much less incentive to work toward that goal. Likewise, as a student, how often were you asked to *repeat* a task or activity over and over again not knowing why? With no idea what was wrong with what we did, how could we ever have known what to do to better it? How could we have possibly fixed what was wrong, improve what was not good enough, or solidify what was inconsistent if we didn't know what that was?

As teachers we don't intentionally keep our students in the dark. I think we either forget to make it a priority or are in such a hurry to get things done that we don't take the time to do it. It is time consuming, but is time well spent. In a classroom, like in a crowded auditorium, I won't—no, I really can't—effectively "run" to a goal unless I know what that goal is and why I'm running there.

Will there be times we repeat an exercise simply to make certain immediate success wasn't luck? Will there be times we repeat the work at hand solely with the goal of developing consistency, context, confidence or comfort? Yes, but why not share those goals with our students, for aren't those reasons as important as any? To me, any goal worth having is one worth sharing. In that way, sharing the *why* as much as the *how* and *what* of our directives toward those goals, students' progress and growth will be ensured.

So the next time you feel the pressure of the clock as you are teaching, and are tempted to skip those moments of sharing the goal as you hurry toward it, doing the educational equivalent of yelling the word "run," remember that auditorium full of people who never even uncrossed their legs.

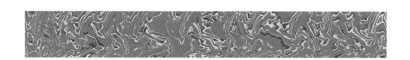

VISION

Fulton Oursler wrote, "Every day man crucifies himself between two thieves — fear of tomorrow and regrets of yesterday." Worse still, that fear and regret is often so debilitating as to obscure the enjoyment of today — the here and now. In so doing it becomes easy to cloak the past, present and future in a haze of negativity, worry and doubt.

As teachers, however, nothing could be more foreign to our way of thinking. For at the heart of education is the premise that we learn from yesterday, savor today and look forward to tomorrow. That we plan as a result of the past, enjoy and truly live the present, and dream of what the future can hold as a consequence. Quite simply, at the core of being a teacher is that mysterious quality called *vision*: the ability to see more than meets the eye.

Vision is a magical mixture of hindsight, foresight, now-sight and insight that is the essence of great teaching. It is that remarkable combination, in just the right proportion, at just the right time, in just the right way that can make all the difference in the lives of those whom we are entrusted to teach. Just like a marvelous recipe for some fabulous dish, the subtle interplay and balance of every ingredient

and cooking technique is seemingly invisible to the unini-
tiated, but in the hands of a master chef can become a
thing of beauty.

Hindsight

Hindsight is simply the ability to look at what has already
occurred, to perceive and examine aspects of previous
events and decisions as they truly happened, and to see
other possibilities or choices that could have been more
appropriate or beneficial. It is basically the ability to objectively assess the past.

Most people think of hindsight in negative terms, with
statements like "in hindsight I would never have bought
that car" or "in hindsight I guess I should have unplugged
the iron." But for teachers, hindsight is a valuable com-
modity. It is essential, for without it we would have no idea
where our students *are*, before starting them on the path to
where they are *going*. Hindsight allows us to establish starting points, it is the fruit of assessment, it is the information
we need to know to help children *bloom where they are planted*.
We are all simply a product of our pasts.

Though in the process of education "what was" can be
viewed with regret and criticism, it is always best to view it
rather as a result; facts as we now know them to be. *What
is*, is. *What was* becomes extraordinarily valuable information we as teachers can use. From that information we can
plan future programs of study, tailor specific lessons, learn
which approaches work and which fail, assess learning
styles, individualize instruction and reflect on our expectations. As teachers, hindsight allows us to live the words of

that wonderful old phrase: "We cannot direct the wind…
but we can adjust the sails."

Hindsight allows us to do just that by assessing what has
occurred as much as learning from it, processing what was as
much as planning what will be, creating the future from our
knowledge of the past. I guess the best analogy for hindsight
is rowing a boat. As we row a boat forward, we face backward,
always looking where we have been, moving ahead based on
what we see behind us. In so doing, moving correctly toward
the future by referencing what has been in our past.

It is said that information is power and much of that
power comes from what we learn from a keenly developed
sense of hindsight.

Foresight

Foresight: the act of looking to the future, providing for
the future, understanding the significance of the future, and
acting upon the present as a *result* of one's view of the future.
Could anything be more "teacher-like"? We look at the past
as a springboard or launch pad to the future. Then, using
foresight, we envision what our students can be and chart
a course for their destiny. In a nutshell, foresight is seeing
potential, dreaming of what can be — not what others *say*
can be — with the only true limitation to those dreams
being *our imagination*. I often think of foresight as being able
to *see even with our eyes closed*: that dreaming, that envisioning
of hidden potential, that seeing what's within each of our
students that is at the very core of being a teacher. What a
wonderful metaphor for teaching. What a wonderful metaphor for so much of life, or more important, living.

As with hindsight, most people think of foresight negatively, with phrases such as "I wish I had the foresight to bring an umbrella." But foresight, true foresight, offers us the opportunity not only to look toward the future as we want it to be, but to create it that way. Foresight allows us to prevent what we *don't* want to happen and to cause or initiate what we *do* want to happen. It allows us to live out of our imagination instead of our *memories*. More important, it allows us to live out of our imagination rather than our *regrets*.

Now-Sight

Tennessee Williams wrote, "Life is all memory, except for the one present moment that goes by you so quickly you hardly catch it going." Don't you think it's true that many of us go through much of our teaching day, let alone our lives, *looking — but not seeing — because our eyes are closed?* How sad it is when we spend so much time and energy worrying about the past or future that we don't enjoy and savor the moment, the here and now, that we don't see what's there, right in front of us.

It's like holding a camera with hopes of taking the quintessential picture. There we are impatiently waiting for the ideal shot, worrying about seizing the right instant, anguishing over opportunities lost. More often than not, though, we spend so much time doing all that, we miss the moment. I don't just mean miss the photograph, I mean miss even seeing — really seeing — the precious scene that just passed unnoticed, unappreciated, unrepeatable.

The problem we teachers have is that we spend so much time focusing on hindsight and foresight that we often don't take the time to live in the moment. Now I know teaching some concepts and skills can be maddeningly frustrating, and the only thing that sometimes "gets us through" is focusing on what possibilities lay ahead for those students after they learn those lessons, but we must enjoy the journey as much as the destination. Finding joy along the path to the goal is, quite possibly, more important than savoring joy once the goal has been achieved.

Jonathan Swift hoped for this when he cautioned, "May you live every day of your life." Buddha sought the same ideal when he reasoned, "If we could see the miracle of a single flower clearly, our whole life would change." But Albert Einstein said it most eloquently: "There are two ways to live your life. One is as though nothing is a miracle. The other is as though everything is a miracle." The miracle of living, the miracle of education, the miracle of growth demand that we honor those words by seeing our "now" as much as our "what was" and "what will be."

I guess now-sight boils down to *seeing* versus *looking*, and we alone determine which we will do, how we will spend our days. One thing's for sure, we can never forget that the same seven letters that create the words "the eyes" make the words "they see," but only if we let them, only if we make them and only if we take the time to do so. Right now—this moment—is not simply the space between the past and the future. It is a brief moment that must be treasured and enjoyed.

Insight

Hindsight is contemplating the past to guide the future. Foresight is envisioning the potential the future holds.

Now-sight is cherishing the present moment, but the most magical of the four "sights" must be the last one: *insight*. Insight is that ability to look at events with intuition, perception and understanding. It is being aware of what motivates students and seeing the underlying truths that govern any situation.

A teacher's insight is part mystic, part pragmatist, part sage, part shaman and part psychologist. Our stock in trade: being as astute as we are ingenious, as skillful as we are clever, possessing judgment as sound as it is nimble. In short it is living the words of William Arthur Ward who said, "The pessimist complains about the wind; the optimist expects it to change; the realist adjusts the sails." As teachers, pessimists wallow in regrets of the past; optimists, without the guidance of information and a plan, hope for improvement; but realists, armed with hindsight and foresight to guide them, can enjoy the now-sight of the present while guiding "the ships" that are our students with the instinct, wisdom and understanding of true insight.

A Teacher's Eyes

For teachers seeing is more than just believing, it's knowing, hoping, envisioning, evaluating, estimating, planning, growing, cajoling, enjoying and calculating. But above all it's simply believing. Believing in the power of education. Believing in the promise of education.

In so doing let us each resolve to live the following words of Napoleon Hill: "Cherish your visions and your dreams as they are the children of your soul; the blueprints of your ultimate achievements." Remembering all the while that sometimes the things you can't see matter most. ▓

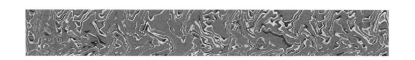

THE REAL VOYAGE

"You see this goblet?" asks Achaan Chaa, the Thai meditation master. "For me this glass is already broken. I enjoy it; I drink out of it. It holds my water admirably, sometimes even reflecting the sun in beautiful patterns. If I should tap it, it has a lovely ring to it. But when I put this glass on the shelf and the wind knocks it over or my elbow brushes it off the table and it falls to the ground and shatters, I say, 'Of course.' When I understand that the glass is already broken, every moment with it is precious."

How many of us — through frustration with where our students *are* versus where we know we want them to be; or because our dedication drives us never to settle, but rather always to push our students to the next step — don't cherish the time we have with our students? That wondrous quote from Mark Epstein's *Thoughts Without A Thinker* puts it all in perspective. Many of us dwell so much on where our students should be by the end of the year, or by test time, making it easy to forget they all too soon will be gone. That wonderful, unique group of individuals will move on in only months, a thought which serves to remind us of how each moment with our students is precious. As the goblet thought of as already broken is treasured, time with our students must be savored.

Put succinctly by H. Schachtel, "Happiness is not having what you want, but rather wanting what you have." I know it's sometimes hard to think of that but we can never be truly happy until we do. Otherwise we will always be waiting for happiness — or that day when we *can* cherish time with our students — sometime in the future. As former President Ronald Reagan stated, "Don't wait until the evening sunset to see the beauty of the day." Work toward that majestically beautiful sunset but enjoy every ray of sun and yes, every storm cloud that passes.

If you only cherish the time with classes that are stellar, or the times that produce great results, you will get to the end of a career with far fewer moments of joy than if you follow those incredible words of Herb Gardner: "You have got to own your days and name them, each one of them, every one of them, or else the years go right by and none of them belong to you." Don't let the years just *go* by. Cherish every second of every day, and name each of them with the smiles of joy or looks of amazement on the faces of those whom you teach. Maybe it is simply realizing that "the real voyage of discovery," as Marcel Proust so perfectly stated, "consists not in seeking new landscapes, but in having new eyes."

Acting on that thought is certainly more of a challenge with some children than with others. Savoring moments with students who seem uninterested or unfocused is hard. It helps to keep in mind the truth of J. R. R. Tolkien's "The Riddle of Aragorn" from *The Fellowship of the Ring*: "Not all those who wander are lost." No one, no matter how wonderful a teacher he or she is, can *always* know whether children who appear to be wandering are really lost. Maybe they are, or maybe they are processing, imagining, extrapolating or analyzing. Just maybe that moment a student *looks* lost could be a moment of revelation: the moment "the light finally went on."

We can be the teacher who nurtures those moments. We can be the teacher who fosters what is truly important in a young person's life. We can be the teacher who sends the true message that every child needs to learn, best stated by the astounding Pablo Casals: "Each second we live in a new and unique moment of the universe, a moment that never was before and will never be again. And what do we teach our children in school? We teach them that two and two make four, and that Paris is the capital of France. When will we also teach them what they are? We should say to each of them: Do you know what you are? You are a marvel. You are unique. In all of the world there is no other child exactly like you. In the millions of years that have passed there has never been another child like you. And look at your body—what a wonder it is! Your legs, your arms, your cunning fingers, the way you move! You may become a Shakespeare, a Michelangelo, a Beethoven. You have the capacity for anything. Yes, you are a marvel. And when you grow up, can you then harm another who is, like you, a marvel? You must cherish one another. You must work—we all must work—to make this world worthy of its children."

Those words of Casals are brilliant; they are also a tall order. How does one even start? For me, I start by trying every day to work toward cherishing and being worthy of the children I teach. Will I ever truly be? Probably not,

but all any of us can do is try. All any of us can do is live
the words of Rachel Carson: "If a child is to keep alive his
inborn sense of wonder, he needs…at least one adult who
can share it, rediscovering with him the joy, excitement
and mystery of the world we live in." We may be the only
adult who does, so we must. A friend of mine once said that
a truly great teacher "always puts the students first, the subject matter second and themselves last."

Is that easy? No, but as Tom Brokaw affirmed, "It's easy to
make a buck. It's a lot harder to make a difference." Think of
those teachers who made a difference in your life. Think of
the true lessons they taught you. For me, every one of them
cared more about me as a person than about anything they
hoped to teach me and worked as hard to make me a better
human being as they did to make me a smarter student.

Mitch Albom in his stunning book, *Tuesdays with Morrie*,
chronicled the life and death of one such teacher of his. I
think we can live no better than to strive to exemplify his
words: "Have you ever really had a teacher? One who saw
you as a raw but precious thing, a jewel that, with wisdom,
could be polished to a proud shine? If you are lucky enough
to find your way to such teachers, you will always find your
way back. Sometimes it is only in your head. Sometimes it
is right alongside their beds. The last class of my old professor's life took place once a week, in his home, by a window
in his study where he could watch a small hibiscus plant
shed its pink flowers. The class met on Tuesdays. No books
were required. The subject was the meaning of life. It was
taught from experience. The teaching goes on."

But how does one *teach* the meaning of life? Well,
by showing and "being" the simple credo of Jonathan

Swift: "May you live all the days of your life." Indeed. May you—and every student whose life you touch—remember to *enjoy* the precious moments shared, *want* what you have, *name* every day, *have* new eyes, *make* a difference, *cherish* one another, and truly *live* all the days of your life. ▨

EVERY PERSON HAS A STORY

"Where are you off to this morning?" asked the young driver as we pulled away from the hotel en route to the airport. "New York City," I replied in a groggy voice, the result of a combination of jet lag and sleep deprivation. "How would you compare Oregon to New York?" he asked inquisitively. Fighting back a yawn, I responded by talking about how both places were wonderful. "I really want to visit New York someday," he stated, "but first I want to go to Japan." Now at 6 a.m., on three hours of sleep, it was hard for me to think, let alone talk, but I wanted to be friendly, so I replied with something like: "That's nice."

He continued with a brief life story: "Well, you see, I was born in California, then moved to Eugene for college, but I have spent a lot of time in Seattle. So because I have spent my life on the West Coast, I feel the need to explore other places. After I graduate, since I am studying Japanese, I want to teach for a year in Tokyo." He went on to speak of his studies, his dreams, his aspirations, his concerns, his fears and his hopes. As he talked, I listened more. As tired as I was, it just seemed so important. He was reaching out and I had to reach back. I forced myself to find the energy to communicate with this stranger whom I would probably never see again. He had a story, and I found myself actively listening to every word, egging him on for more. Fatigue lost out to connecting with a fellow human being.

By now I am sure you are thinking this story will turn to one where he tells me he was the victim of some terrible tragedy or he was suffering from an incurable disease. Nope. No talk of suicide or domestic violence. Nothing profound, devastating or bizarre. I'm certain that if the conversation had taken that turn I would have listened and communicated with all my heart. I would have counseled and commiserated with every fiber of my being. Isn't that what we teachers always do? But it didn't turn. This was just simple chatting about everyday life but I listened intently and thoughtfully. I wanted him to feel that I was interested. Truthfully, at first I was far more concerned with closing my eyes for twenty minutes on the way to the airport. But sharing time with that polite young man became important. Why? I don't know. I do know that I didn't want to let him down or make him think I was uninterested.

We arrived at the airport, he handed me my luggage, and wished me a safe trip. I wished him well for his future. And as he walked away, he said, "I hope I see you again sometime." You know what, so did I. As I walked into the airport and wandered to my gate, a bad feeling came over me. I couldn't shake it but I also couldn't understand it. It was a combination of disappointment with myself, regret, opportunity lost, and introspection. In short, it was the feeling I get when I am *not* being the teacher I want to be or hope I can be. I was plagued by it but didn't understand why that simple conversation with a stranger would make me feel that way. It obviously hit a nerve and got me thinking about it in relation to my teaching. What could that possibly have to do with my being a better teacher?

Then, standing in line to board the airplane it hit me. What troubled me was that I took the time and energy to do that with a total stranger but hadn't taken the time and energy to do that with every one of the students entrusted to me. I knew in my heart that when students came to me with a problem or crisis I attended to them. When a death in the family, illness or divorce struck I would take the time to talk. When a crisis of career choice or ability came to a head I would try to reach out. When a relationship broke up I would offer sympathy. That was not the problem.

What bothered me so much was my knowing that unless it was a crisis, I was not always willing to make time just to chat. About everything or nothing. Truthfully, I didn't know if my students wanted to teach in Tokyo or if any of them took Japanese. But I knew that about a young man whom I met for twenty minutes some 3,000 miles across the country. On a practical level, I understood that part of the problem was time. I could certainly rationalize my concerns with a formula that went something like this: time equals the number of students I have, divided by the number of hours in a day, minus personal life crises, multiplied by the square root of the ever-present feeling of being away from my family too much, added to the inverse of the sum total of time spent doing paperwork, answering the phone, responding to email and attending meetings. Time just seems so elusive. Maybe time couldn't be found. But I knew

I always found time when a student was rushed to the hospital, or for a student's brother's funeral, or to help a student who I feared would take his or her own life. Why was there not enough time just to chat? That conundrum seemed to be the quintessential example of *not* living life as if there were no tomorrows. I knew that formula was just a reasonable excuse and remembered a wonderful quote a friend gave to me: "Excuses are the nails to build a house of failure."

I hope, no, I pray my students know I care about them. Not just about their education but about their lives, about them as people. I know they mean so very much to me but do they know it? I think being there for them at times of distress is very important. Being there for guidance and counsel is as well. But the truth be known, I think the crisis of conscience I had at the airport reflects the fact that I think spending more time just chatting may be equally important.

I then realized this must be something I am very concerned about. Why else would it have disturbed me so? Enough negative, I thought. I was going to seize the opportunity. I needed to take positive steps, to move forward, to do and to be better. I had to live those words of William Drayton, "Change starts when someone sees the next step." Thinking about how this all began I decided that the next day, a Monday morning, as I walked through the halls of my building I would turn over a new leaf of chatting more. Instead of simply saying "hello" when I saw one of my students walk down the hallway, I would chat.

Well all I can tell you is that by about eleven o'clock that Monday morning I overheard one of my students asking a bunch of others, "Why is Dr. Boonshaft asking everybody what language they're taking?" Hey, it was a start. Was it easy? No, I guess I'm not a natural born chit-chatter. It was a challenge. But as Joshua J. Marine asserted, "Challenges are what make life interesting; overcoming them is what makes life meaningful."

Over time I moved on to more lucid chitchat. I like to think I am better at it now. Am I a model of what I would hope to be? No! Am I better? Yes! Many of my students did ask, "What's up?" I never told them. I thought it better just to do it. But if I had answered, what I would have wanted to say was, "Every person has a story. I just wanted to make sure I found out what yours was." To put it simply, I have always wanted to be a teacher who lived by the words of Frederick L. Collins: "There are two types of people — those who come into a room and say, 'Well, here I am!' and those who come in and say, 'Ah, there you are.'"

When I get so busy I fall off the chatting wagon, I think of that young man from Oregon. I wonder if he knows he made me a better teacher on that early morning drive. But even more important, do my students feel I became a better teacher? I hope so. By the way, most of them took Spanish.

WRESTLING A GORILLA

"Genius," wrote Thomas Edison, "is one percent inspiration and ninety-nine percent perspiration." Have you ever thought about that renowned quote? I mean truly *thought* about it, not just *heard* it? The "inspiration" part is straightforward enough, but what did he really mean by "perspiration"? Is it simply hard work? Probably so, but don't you think the effort he refers to must also include a healthy dose of perseverance? I can't help but believe Mr. Edison would have thought so. Perseverance, that resolve and determination to continue in the face of frustration, fatigue, resistance, obstacles, difficulty or failure, is quite certainly at the core of genius, but more important, it is at the very heart of teaching and learning.

Have you ever had one of those classes where nothing seemed to go right? You know, the ones which test your ability as much as your patience, where achievement seems distant and the chances of success in reaching your goal seem remote. On those occasions, students seem unmovable, unwilling to budge despite our best efforts. It's like trying to move a mountain or drag a donkey. It's quite simply like a wrestling match of will, patience and stamina, stated

best by Robert Strauss when he advised, "Perseverance is
a little like wrestling a gorilla. You don't quit when you're
tired, you quit when the gorilla is tired."

We all have those days, yet we all know tomorrow holds
the promise of better. So we persevere, knowing the cause
is too vital and the work too important to do anything less.
We live the words of Publius who declared, "I can live with
losing the good fight, but I can not live without fighting it."
We practice the words of Margaret Thatcher who warned,
"You may have to fight a battle more than once to win it."
We heed the words of Cervantes who realized, "He who
loses wealth loses much; he who loses a friend loses more;
but he that loses courage loses all."

Whether it is the courage to persevere in the face of
obstacles, the temporary failures of the moment, the difficulties of a situation, or the apprehension of an unplanned
educational detour, it is the courage to persevere that can
make all the difference in the lives of those whom we teach.
It may mean having the courage to stay the course, adapt our
approach, savor a tangent, remediate a problem, learn from
a mistake or delight in an unexpected revelation. It may be
any or all of those things; the only constant is courage.

Though remembering thoughts like those can help
keep things in perspective, sometimes it's still a bumpy ride
on the road of progress. Sometimes teaching feels like we
are running at full speed straight into the wind. At those
times the trick is to realize that in many ways our success
in teaching is like an airplane on takeoff. That's right, an
airplane on takeoff. Let me explain.

It would seem that our teaching would be best, most
fruitful, when all is going as planned, students are with us

and the proverbial wind is at our backs. Just like it would seem that the best chance for an airplane to lift from earth would be for it to have the wind at its back, helping to move it aloft. Not so. Not so at all. In fact, nothing could be further from the truth. You see, airplanes always take off *into* the wind. It's true: pilots steer their crafts straight into as much headwind as they can. Why? Bernoulli.

More precisely, the Bernoulli Effect, which tells us that lift is created by the pressure differential above and below the airfoil shape of a wing. So the more air that runs across a wing—coming from that headwind—the better. Strange as it may seem, the more wind we get in our face, truly forcing our airplane into the path of most resistance, the easier we can soar to great heights. Maybe that's true in teaching as well?

Maybe those times when we need to wrestle gorillas can be more productive than we think, as long as we keep at it until the gorillas are tired. Maybe having the educational "wind" in our face can be stimulating and invigorating. Maybe our best teaching can be found on the path of *most* resistance. Maybe our teaching challenges are the "headwind" we need for our educational "lift." Maybe, just maybe, wrestling gorillas can be more wonderful, more joyous, more amazing than one could ever imagine.

Bel Kaufman, in her splendid book, *Up the Down Staircase,* offers a poignant glimpse into the essence of perseverance. Threaded through the book are notes written back and forth between a new teacher and an experienced colleague about the frustrations of education. The new teacher, after many trying experiences, wrote, "I am—more than a bit fed up. I once taught a lesson on 'A man's reach should exceed his grasp, or what's a heaven for?' I'm no longer sure that this is so; the higher I reach, the flatter I fall on my face. How do you manage to stand up?"

The response from her experienced friend, brought to her by a student, is as overpowering in its simplicity as it is in its truth: "Look at the cherub who is delivering this note. Look closely. Did you ever see a lovelier smile? A prouder bearing? She has just made the Honor Society. Last year she was ready to quit school. Walk through the halls. Listen at the classroom doors. In one—a lesson on the nature of Greek tragedy. In another—a drill on *who* and *whom*. In another—a hum of voices intoning French conjugations. In another—committee reports on slum clearance. In another—silence: a math quiz. Whatever…something very exciting is going on. In each of the classrooms, on each of the floors, all at the same time, education is going on. In some form or other…young people are exposed to education. That's how I manage to stand up. And that's why you're standing too."

Each time I read those glorious words, each time I am reminded of that stirring quote by Browning referenced by the young teacher, I realize its truth and wisdom. We each must cherish our strength to persevere, to stand and face the wind, to reach beyond our grasp, to know the power of education and the promise of our mission. In that way for us as teachers our reach will always exceed our grasp, and that my friends is just what a heaven is for. So the next time those gorillas show up with thoughts of wrestling, embrace the possibilities and realize the importance. ▰

"We'll Make It Fun"

There I was at a state education conference, sitting outside a large exhibition hall. I was taking a break, relaxing quietly, when all of a sudden the all-state chorus came walking by en masse. It turns out the students, all three hundred of them, were given this time to spend walking around the exhibits. Now I love doing that and I think it is a great idea, but I did hear several kids complaining the whole way in. The laments were strong and numerous.

That was until a group of young ladies walked by me. Instead of joining the chorus (sorry, I couldn't resist) of grumpy voices griping about this plan, one of them said, "It's okay, we'll make it fun."

I was shocked. No, I was flabbergasted. I don't know why, but in this day and age to hear a young person with sparkling optimism was so very wonderful. And for you cynics reading this, she wasn't being sarcastic. She really meant it. I marveled as I watched and listened to this charming young woman convince her friends to make this event a positive one. She could have just as easily gone with the pack and complained her way through the time, but she didn't. She chose to make it fun.

Now the truth be known, she could have meant that they were going to burn the building down or trip old people for fun, but I doubt it. She didn't just say those words, she sold them. After they passed I sat there trying to figure out what made her that way. What made her say that and really mean it? I don't know, but I guess she was a product of her teachers and her parents. She must have learned it somewhere, and that somewhere was probably by seeing others say and do the same.

What a wonderful way to go through life: choosing to make boring or lackluster situations positive and worthwhile, yes even fun. Now before you start expecting smiley faces and rainbows on the next page assuming I have lost my charter membership in the Pessimists Club, I'm the first one to say that some things are never going to be fun no matter how you slice them. Getting a tooth drilled or having a flat tire is never going to be fun, never.

But how about some of the more tedious or tiresome things we must teach? Do we make them fun for our students? Do we show enjoyment even when confronted with frustration? Certainly I know I can't always be happy or always make things fun but I wonder if I could do it more than I do. After stewing about that young lady's words I started thinking of all the times I could have made my teaching more fun if I had only thought of her advice.

What a wonderful lesson for each of us: simply seizing every opportunity to make things not only hopeful and valuable, but fun, whenever we can, wherever we can, especially during those times that don't seem to be so. Now I hear her words every time I see boring and mundane around the corner, wondering how it can be made to be fun. I figure

that if our students see us live those words, they too will
learn that lesson, and what a wonderful gift that would be. ▨

THE FOREST FOR
THE TREES

The football field runs north and south at our local high
school, the home team bleachers standing high on the
east side of the field, facing west. When I had all three of
my children in the high school marching band, one of my
favorite things to do each fall was to occasionally go to the
school and watch an evening rehearsal. It just felt wonderful:
the crisp air, the turning leaves, the sound of a drum cadence
and the pride I felt watching my kids. I can't explain the joy
but I guess some things just can't be explained.

However, being a music teacher I can't help but pri-
vately critique, analyze and evaluate everything I see and
hear. I don't want to but I can't help it. I find myself focusing
on every flaw. I listen for every wrong note and problem. I
watch for every misstep and gaffe. I myopically concentrate
on the smallest of errors in an almost vicarious attempt to
attend to every detail of the performance.

One such evening, I watched as the band was working diligently on its show. Being very early in the season,
it was, quite frankly, pretty rough at times. There were

lots of mistakes and much frustration. It seemed that even though I was fiercely concentrating, my telepathic efforts just weren't working. I was as frustrated as the kids and their teacher. With the patience of a saint, this wonderful educator would tell the kids to go back to a certain point in the routine and work through the set, always offering constructive criticism and praise. But let's face it, doing that over and over again, no matter how much praise is heaped on, can still have everyone seeing each error as if larger than life.

After the kids returned to their starting places facing the stands for another repetition, all of a sudden a very different command came out of the mouth of this teacher. With a firm yet joyful voice she said, "Everybody turn around and take a minute to appreciate the beautiful sunset." At that moment, as the students turned around, I looked up from the field to see one of the most magical, magnificent sunsets I have ever seen. The sky was ablaze with shades of red and yellow and orange that lit the evening sky with indescribable beauty.

There in front of my eyes I saw something even more beautiful than that sunset. I saw a teacher, a real teacher. For you see, I was so preoccupied with every flaw, concentrating on each wrong note, that I failed to see the spectacular sight before me. I was staring due west that entire time and never saw the forest for the trees. All I had to do was look up and notice. Sadder still, if I were their teacher that night, I don't think I would have told the students to do that, not because I wouldn't have wanted to, but because I probably wouldn't have noticed it.

On that fall evening, sitting in the stands of a football field, I learned a wonderful lesson from that amazing teacher. She heard every mistake and saw every foible, but would never — no *could* never — miss an opportunity to share beauty with those whom she was entrusted to teach. Wonder is all around us; I guess the trick is to always be looking for it, especially when it's right in front of us.

As I write these words I am on an airplane flying from San Jose to Las Vegas. I am also realizing just how hard it is to teach an old dog new tricks. For you see I have been so preoccupied with writing these words, tapping away on my computer, that I failed to take notice of the regal mountains that connect California with Nevada which have been in plain sight just outside my window for the past hour. Only at the end of my flight did I glance up and happen upon the sight. The snow-capped beauty, rugged simplicity, vibrant majesty all mine for the taking if I had simply noticed sooner. It was a wonderful chance to gaze at remarkable splendor, sadly lost because I just didn't take the time to see it.

I wonder how many opportunities I have missed to notice astounding sights as I have passed through life. But even more worrisome, I wonder how many opportunities I have missed to point out beauty to my students. How many sunsets have I missed? How many mountains have I failed to share with my students? I hope to do better for myself and my students. I have vowed to remember the lesson I was taught sitting on those bleachers and work hard to live it.

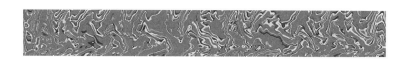

PERSONALITY

"It doesn't matter what brings a person, only what they leave with." So goes the wisdom of a wonderful Irish proverb. As teachers it really doesn't matter what brings students to us as much as the person they find when they get there. That person — that personality — who will capture their minds, spirits, imaginations and hearts: their teacher.

It has been said that teaching is ten percent ability and ninety percent personality, and though that is surely an oversimplification, it does make the point we all know: the great teachers in our lives were somehow always able to connect with us, having personalities that were as powerful as they were sincere, as magnetic as they were concerned. Often that *power of personality* is what brought truth to the notion that the most important thing we as teachers make is a difference.

I often find myself thinking of those teachers in my life who made that difference, those beacons of inspiration, those models of the teacher I rarely am but the teacher I always hope to be. I dwell on their talents. I obsess over their methods. I detail their techniques but when all is said

and done it always seems to be their personality that somehow made me want to learn. As Barbara Harrell Carson so
eloquently stated, "Students learn what they care about,
from people they care about and who, they know, care
about them."

Certainly we can't enumerate all the qualities that make
for a remarkable teacher or diminish the importance of
vast knowledge and exceptional talent, but we simply can't
underestimate the value of that indescribable characteristic
known as *personality*. As Carl Jung so beautifully wrote, "An
understanding heart is everything in a teacher, and cannot
be esteemed highly enough. One looks back with appreciation to the brilliant teachers, but with gratitude to those
who touched our human feeling. The curriculum is so much
necessary raw material, but warmth is the vital element for
the growing plant and for the soul of the child."

For some students it may be their teacher's passion for
the subject matter, effervescence of spirit, enthusiasm for
teaching or excitement about the joys of learning. For other
students it may be their teacher's inviting manner, infectious humor, understated intensity or indomitable commitment. For others still, it will be facets of their teacher's
personality no words can describe. The only commonality
I have ever found — the only one that really matters — in
all of those teachers in my life was their ability to lift up
their students with the sheer strength of their personality as
much as their talent, knowledge and ability.

For many young people it will be their teacher's profound guidance, embodying the words of Lao-Tzu who
affirmed: "To lead the people, walk behind them." Or
their teacher's modeling the wisdom found in the words of

Hermann Hesse when he asserted: "Happiness is a how, not a what; a talent, not an object." Or witnessing their teacher truly embrace the dignity of the phrase, "A different world cannot be built by indifferent people."

Maybe it's just that gift teachers have of being able to understand the student inside every person and the person inside every student. Maybe it's simply a teacher's capacity to care more than seems logical. Or maybe it's something only a teacher knows and a student senses. But whatever that mysterious thing we call personality *is*, however we try to describe it, one thing's for sure: it can make all the difference in the life of a child. A difference no words can describe short of paraphrasing the old adage: For those who understand, no explanation is necessary, for those who do not, none will suffice. ▨

ONE SIMPLE QUESTION

After finishing a day of offering workshop sessions as part of a summer conference, I found myself in front of a small auditorium full of teachers, the focus of an open forum to close the day's activities. You know, where participants can ask questions on any topic that interests them. I usually love those opportunities to share with my colleagues, finding that I learn far more from *their* questions than I can offer with *my* answers. Sometimes those questions can be straightforward and answered with simple facts. Sometimes they can be so open-ended as to allow only broad generalities. Sometimes they are thought-provoking probes seeking an opinion about questions I fear have no finite answer.

At that moment, however, I was asked a question that was nothing short of mind-boggling. I don't just mean it was a fact I didn't know or a topic I was clueless about. That happens all the time and I just plead ignorance. This was different. This one took my breath away with a physical reaction akin to panic. Why? Because this was a question for which I *had* to have an answer, an answer that governed all I do as a teacher. The question was at once as simple as it was weighty, as complicated as it was formidable, as amazing as it was daunting. What was it, you ask? It was simply, "Dr. Boonshaft, what is the single most important thing we can do as teachers?"

After I caught my breath and stopped trembling at the magnitude of the query, my reaction was to ask if they would rather I tackle an easier question like the solution for global warming or the formula for peace on earth. Because, quite frankly, I think I may have had a better shot at answering those questions. Instead, I sat quietly, thinking as hard as I could while looking out at the sea of eyes, those thoughtful souls waiting to hear my opinion. It *was* a great question; I only wish I had a great answer. But I didn't.

The minute I took to ponder the question seemed to last forever. It felt like an eternity as I reflected on possible answers. Was it to help students learn how to learn or to empower young people with tools for life and living? Was it to help children to reach their potential or to light a fire of curiosity in all those whom we teach? Was it to help students find beauty in the world or to become well-rounded individuals? Was it to help society by planting seeds for future generations or cultivating human beings more in touch with their souls? Was it to help young people express themselves? At that moment my problem was that all of those answers and a myriad of others were correct. Yes, I thought, we need to do all of those things.

So I took a deep breath and rattled off a longwinded reply which included much of the above. As I finished my response, confident I had dodged that bullet, the gentleman who asked the question replied, "I asked for the *single* most important thing, not a list of things." Needless to say at that point I heard bullets whizzing by my head in every direction! So I thought a bit more as the audience sat patiently waiting for me to further make a fool of myself. At that instant, like a bad movie, memories of the great teachers in my life flooded my mind. I saw their faces, and more important, I felt their presence. Or better put, I felt how they always made me feel.

What was it about them? Was it how much they knew? No, I had many teachers who knew more. Was it simply that they cared about me? No, for I surely had other teachers who cared more. Was it how much they pushed me to achieve? No, others did that even more. Then it hit me. I had my answer.

I took another deep breath, this time with great satisfaction, smiled knowingly, looked out at my inquisitor and said, "I think the single most important thing we can do as teachers is *to make every single student feel he or she is incredibly important.*" How did I arrive at that seemingly simple answer? Well as I thought about all of those remarkable teachers in my life, yes, they knew a great deal, cared about me and pushed me to achieve, but there was something more, something far greater.

It was simply that in their presence I felt special, important and valued. They made me feel I really mattered and *that* feeling made me work harder, learn more and fulfill that perception as best I could. How did they communicate that feeling? I have no idea, but I do know that with each word or action they sent the message loud and clear, reinforcing it over and over again. But as I reflect back on those teachers, the most amazing thing isn't just that they were able to make *me* feel that way, it was that they were able to make *every* student in their class feel that way—every single one.

It reminded me of my mom; more specifically an event shortly after her passing. My mother was an extraordinary person. Her kindness and warmth radiated with a sincerity I have rarely witnessed. She had a way of making everyone she met feel special and valued in a way I can't describe. I knew she had this ability, for surely I grew up nurtured by it, but I never appreciated it more than the day of her funeral. At the end of the service, in a receiving line, my family greeted those who came to pay their respects to this kind woman. One by one, Mom's friends offered their condolences and told their favorite story or recollection.

The most wonderful part, however, was that so many people, after looking around to make certain no one could hear them, whispered to us that they were my mom's *best* friend. At the end of that day, as my sister and I reflected back upon those conversations, we marveled at our mother's ability to make everyone—every single person—feel extremely important. It was real, it was true, it was sincere. She never needed to fake it or pretend because to her people were special. She could find joyous qualities and importance in just about anyone, and that couldn't help but make people feel like they were her best friend. You know what, truth be known, each of them probably was her best friend. That's just how amazing she was.

That quality, that virtue, that special ability was shared by all of the great teachers in my life who, each in their own way, made me feel so very important. They went far beyond just providing a sense of happiness or comfort; they empowered me, encouraged me and emboldened me. They made me part of a prophecy they each saw that I couldn't help but work to prove true. It was a gift I cherished back then. It is a goal I have tried to make real in my teaching now. For surely students who are made to believe they are incredibly important can and will achieve just about anything.

I wish I could say I have succeeded in making every student feel that important; I have not. I haven't even come close, but I do try as hard as I can because I know how very important it is. Truly, what could be more important? Maybe people, like those great teachers, like my mom, are born that way, and I will never be able to meet that challenge. But I know what it meant to me and I hope to honor each of those marvelous influences in my life — and honor each of my students — by trying. A simple question indeed. ▓

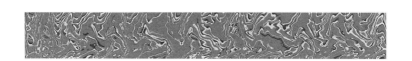

MISTAKES?

Mistakes are bad. Right? Isn't that what we tell our students or at least imply to them and to ourselves? Writing the word "their" where it should have been "there" is a mistake. The answer "nine" as the sum of three plus three is a mistake. Stating that "Michigan is the capital of Cleveland" is a mistake. True? Well, yes and no.

If correctness is the *only* measure our students or we learn to use then the answer is "yes." But if that is the case, little will be discovered, uncovered or explored. In other words, doing what we know that works, *repeating* what's been done without error, may make the world *go around*, but *mistakes* make it *go forward*. What better lesson can we teach our students and how better can we show it than by example?

Don't get me wrong, I'm not saying that mistakes should be ignored or accepted. Not at all, but they should not be fatal to the learning process. Yes, there are times when wrong is wrong and that's it, but there are often times when wrong can be magnificent, wrong can be an opportunity for new possibilities, and wrong can expand our horizons.

As teachers, and more important, as learners, we need to develop both abilities: the skill to replicate and the capacity to create. On the one hand we want our students to replicate *what is known* with fewer and fewer errors. The goal then is to demonstrate their abilities as well as possible, reproduce success, copy excellence, imitate correctness, repeat for improvement and practice for consistency. Here mistakes are bad, problematic and unwanted.

On the other hand we want our students to create *what can be* with unconstrained enthusiasm and uninhibited abandon. The goal then is to create, originate, produce and envision what doesn't exist, whether it's devising improvements to what has already been done or conceiving innovative ideas about what has *never* been done. Here mistakes can be joyous fuel for a wildfire of creativity.

By way of example, name a few of the most famous towers in the world. I'll bet somewhere on your list was the Leaning Tower of Pisa. Why? Why is it so famous? Without a doubt, it is among the most famous buildings in the world not just *despite* but *because* of the mistake of its leaning to the side. By any builder's standard that is a mistake, but it is seen as beautiful and amazing to all those who behold it. I wonder if we would know of that tower in the town of Pisa if not for its odd sense of what's vertical. My guess is no. But the world has one more marvel in it because of that mistake.

Similarly, if I asked you to name some of the most successful inventions in office supplies in the past few decades, undoubtedly *Post-it Notes* would be high on the list. They have in many ways revolutionized office communication. They are everywhere, in every size, color and shape imaginable. Certainly whoever invented them didn't make a mistake. Or did he?

You see those sticky little yellow sheets of paper we all have on our desks began as a scientist's experiment. What was he trying to discover, you ask? Surely it must have been the weakest glue imaginable, the most temporary of adhesives. Wrong; his goal was to invent the strongest glue possible. That's right, the ultimate permanent bonding agent. How's that for a whopper of a mistake?

Here's how it happened. Spencer Silver, a research scientist with the 3M Corporation, was working on inventing a new, stronger, permanent glue. The result of one of his attempts was a glue that was just about the opposite of his goal. What he came up with was a glue that was not at all strong and not the least bit permanent. In fact he invented as weak and temporary a glue as one could imagine.

Some years later a gentleman by the name of Art Fry, another employee of 3M who knew of Silver's mistaken invention, had what turned out to be a pretty darned good idea while singing in his church choir. Each week, as the story goes, Mr. Fry used paper bookmarks to help keep his place in the hymnal, a strategy which worked well when they didn't *fall out of the book*. Then in a moment of what turned out to be sheer brilliance, Fry remembered the mistakenly invented glue he had heard about all those years earlier. The rest, as they say, is history.

So whether it's a tower in Italy, the little sticky notes on your desk or mistakes made every day in classrooms, they can lead to beauty, wonder, progress, courage, innovation and growth if we foster the mindset to allow that to happen. We can do just that by creating an environment that encourages students to attempt what they cannot do, as well as to experiment with new ideas using what they can already do. In that way we empower students with the confidence to try without fear of failure as we encourage them to brainstorm and create without fear of ridicule. That freedom, that educational safety and security, can't help but bolster our students' willingness to expose themselves creatively, take imaginative risks and think productively.

With freedom to fail, or maybe better said, *with encouragement to fail*, students will have an entirely different attitude toward mistakes. Think about your own life. What would you have done differently if you had no fear of making mistakes? Would you have tried more experiments or accepted bolder challenges for yourself? Would you have worried less and envisioned more? Would you have savored creating what has never been, as much as recreating what was? Would your creativity have been stifled less and excited more?

Now think about students who are asked to write a poem, recite a monologue or draw a picture. They must decide to put themselves in a most vulnerable position. A positive environment can make them comfortable enough to attempt just about anything they conjure up, armed with a personal philosophy that failure is at the very least evidence of trying, and that simply trying is, in many ways, automatically succeeding. They are then as willing to learn something new as they are eager to experiment and create anew, living those words of General Douglas MacArthur: "Life is a lively process of becoming."

An unhealthy environment, however, may leave them gripped by fear. To those students, mistakes wait around every corner. They are so afraid of their mistakes of commission, ones which result from attempting something and "failing," that they often end up making more mistakes of omission, those made from simply not trying anything at all.

I guess it all comes down to the fact that educational security can be a great teacher, as motivational as it is inspirational, whereas fear can be a terrible teacher, as debilitating as it is inhibiting. But with our help, our fostering a culture of confidence, our students can learn to conquer those fears and choose the path of taking educational risks over fearful stasis. Can that sometimes be a tough choice, especially for a young person? Does a willingness to try and create have its pitfalls? Would it be safer and easier to sit back and wait for others to blaze that creative path? Of course, but what students will soon learn is that taking those risks, educationally gambling on themselves, leading those creative expeditions is always better than following. Sure, you may smash into a tree or trip over a rock as you make your way along that trail, but you will be the first to see the vista at the top of the climb, unobstructed by anyone or anything. A view that is breathtaking for more reasons than meet the eye.

Quite simply, what I hope our students can embrace through their successes and their setbacks is embodied in a phrase, usually attributed to Søren Kierkegaard, that my father taught me when I was very young. In fact it was the guiding philosophy of his life and through him has become so for me as well. Not a day goes by that I can't hear my dad's voice reminding me: "Life is a mystery to be lived, not a problem to be solved." It is a phrase I treasure. It is a phrase that affirms a healthy relationship with failure as much as it looks optimistically toward success. A phrase as much about the perspective of what has been as it is the promise of what will be. A phrase that frames a life of optimistic wonder, creativity, curiosity and an attitude that enjoying the journey is as important as the destination.

We all know that balancing expectations of mastering material without errors on one hand, and aspirations of creating and envisioning without boundaries on the other hand, can be a challenge. But let us never forget the rewards that balancing act can produce for us, for our students and for our world, for now and for the future, for this generation and for generations to come. Am I overstating the case? I don't know; let's ask the student who someday creates a cure, solves an educational problem, composes a masterpiece, envisions the resolution to a legal dispute, designs a better town plan, conceives of a safer way to build bridges, establishes a remarkable charity, or resolves family disputes with inspired vision. All that and a whole lot more from simple mistakes.

By the way, isn't it strangely coincidental that the notes I wrote to myself for this chapter were jotted down on a bunch of *Post-it Notes*? Hmm...

GUARANTEED SUCCESS

Years ago, as he was leaving my office on his way to a final exam, a student said to me, "You'll have to excuse me, I have an appointment with success." I have always remembered those words and the confident smile that beamed from his face. Young people like that allow no limits to what they can learn or who they can become. Sadly I have also had those students who not just predict failure but determine it before they even start a task. For them, daring to dream is tempered by clouds of self-doubt, and risk is an uncomfortable gamble seldom taken. "And the trouble is," as Erica Jong so powerfully warned, "if you don't risk anything, you risk even more." Basically, it often seems that optimistic students think it's challenging to do the impossible while pessimistic students think it's impossible to do the challenging. But why?

Why do successful people believe they will succeed in most anything they undertake? What is the genesis of that kind of confidence, a confidence born out of far more than simple wishful thinking? Confidence for them is so deeply rooted in their being that failure is rarely even considered an option, let alone a probable outcome. Conversely, why do others seemingly assume failure from the start of any task, believing failure is not just a remote possibility but a foregone conclusion?

Why *do* some people see a goal as doable or achievable while others see the same goal as failure just waiting to happen? Are successful individuals simply born more confident and optimistic or is that a learned response? Over time, have they been conditioned by themselves and others to believe they can jump the hurdles of their goals and objectives simply because past attempts have proven they can? Essentially, has each successive achievement left them with no other conclusion than that accomplishing the goal at hand is assured?

Likewise, will numerous failed efforts condition some to assume the worst in all they attempt? Is that the learned response of those who have met with disappointment far too often? Is the enemy of their *success* simply their being *convinced* of their *failure*? When that happens, do they basically set out to prove themselves correct: rationalizing a self-fulfilling prophecy they understand and can control?

As educators we can delight in the joy of teaching young people who believe themselves a success as they begin working toward any new objective, their enthusiasm for every new task sparked by their confidence. They are so sure of a positive outcome they welcome the work which lies ahead. But as wonderful as that is, little can be as heart-breaking as watching young people who are convinced of failure before they even make an attempt at a task.

What can we do? Can the firmly entrenched conditioning of a naysayer's past be changed? Can we as teachers alter the destiny of those who believe failure is their lot in life? Well I'm no psychologist, but surely I think we can help by embracing the brilliant words of Abraham Maslow who so superbly stated, "What is necessary to change a person is to change his awareness of himself." Specifically, our students' *awareness of themselves* as either succeeding at what they set out to do or failing at all they attempt.

Though plain old "good teaching," reinforcing positive behaviors, individualized instruction, programmed learning and self-guided discovery go a long way toward nourishing the psyche of every child — and will serve the majority of our students well — for those few who have convinced themselves of their unquestionable failure, the remedy may be as simple as retraining them that success can be achieved by actually having them succeed, especially during those crucial initial steps toward a goal.

One of my favorite ways to do that goes beyond setting appropriate goals, individualizing objectives, creating accessibly small initial tasks or adding numerous steps along the way to make the progress seem easier. It doesn't just *include* students in setting objectives; it actually makes *them* arrive at the initial steps they will take toward that objective. No doubt for some students we will need to dictate those steps, ensuring their appropriateness, but other times having students make those early decisions can be the spark which helps move them along the path to self-confidence.

When that is the case, after clearly describing a new short-term goal to students and sharing its value, we can discuss and describe many different steps that will lead them toward accomplishing that end. Unquestionably, the *smaller* the *size* of the steps we suggest, the *larger* the *number* of possible steps we offer and the *greater* the *variety* of different approaches to accomplishing the task, the better.

Then, having armed students with a great number of possibilities, we ask them to write down the first two tasks they will undertake at the start of their educational journey. By having students individually determine the first two steps toward the goal, they are allowed to create objectives they know they can accomplish as they begin to take ownership of the work at hand, and ultimately their destiny.

By empowering students to choose the initial steps, those steps may be smaller than we wish, or easier than we wish, but they will usually be achievable. For it is the rare student who will choose a task he or she can't do. Yes, we will have to guard against those few overenthusiastic, overly ambitious or impatient children who will set impossible initial sights, setting themselves up for failure, but most students will be far more cautious than zealous.

The essence of this plan is that each student, with our guidance, will make those first steps small enough and easy enough as to be certain he or she can do them, thus ensuring success. It's as simple as that. After a while of doing this, students will start to feel the pride of accomplishing tasks and begin to feel they can succeed. Success will beget success. Accomplishment will beget accomplishment. If I am convinced I will fail, because I always have, what better start could there be toward reconditioning me than to have me succeed, and what better way to do that than have *me* decide the first two steps; steps I know I can accomplish?

Will this work for every child or for every goal? No, but when the situation is right it can plant seeds of confidence and positive self-determination for those in need of proving to *themselves* they can succeed. Will there be setbacks? Of course. But as Ralph Waldo Emerson reminds us, "Our greatest glory is not in never failing, but in rising up every time we fail." I guess for those pessimistic learners the trick is getting them to envision success as an option, let alone a probable outcome.

For many young people, like most of us, it's often not the goal we set that gets the better of us but the steps we take to reach that goal, especially those crucial initial steps. Remember, "Nobody trips over mountains. It is the small pebble that causes you to stumble. Pass all the pebbles in your path and you will find you will have crossed the mountain." Whether we choose the steps taken toward an objective, or our students help choose them, if those tasks are easy enough that students know they can "step over" those pebbles of learning, before they know it those mountains of education will be behind them and they will be convinced of Virgil's simple observation: We can because we think we can.

Kurt Vonnegut, Jr. stated, "We are what we imagine ourselves to be." We can apply that remarkable sentiment to our teaching as either a warning about students who doom themselves to failure because that is what they imagine themselves to be, or as a harbinger of success for those students who can imagine themselves in no other way. We just have to get each student to understand, paraphrasing the words of George Eliot, that it's *never too late* to become the person you could have been.

THE RIGHT TOOL
FOR THE JOB

Though educational trends, jargon, methods, buzzwords, approaches, techniques, materials and technology seem to continually change, some fundamental truths remain fixtures in teaching and — more important — in learning. Yes, we have developed new technologies to encourage students to practice, new materials for reinforcing concepts, new philosophies of how to assess learning, new ways to accommodate different learning styles, new designs for merging diverse educational content, and the like.

But when it comes to the business of getting a child to be able to physically do something new, the initial learning of how to do a new activity or technique, I always come back to a brief moment I had in a class many decades ago while in undergraduate school. "Just remember," my professor said, "no matter how complicated we try to make it, it all boils down to the fact that we really have only three ways to *teach* a child *how* to do something: trial and error, verbal or written instructions, and imitation." The older I get the truer those words seem. It may be too simplistic, but so is the wheel, and that's worked out pretty well. The trick, to me, is using the most appropriate of those for any given situation, using as many of them as possible and understanding the benefits and shortcomings of each. After all, the wheel is a magnificent device but probably not the best choice as a tool for getting to the moon.

Verbal and written instructions allow us to codify—step by step—how a student will learn a new action or concept, making certain all necessary steps are included and are in the best sequence. Written instructions also allow our directions to be followed even when students are working on their own. Instructions are logical, orderly, neat, precise and easy to use and monitor. Instructions are ideal in many situations and for those reasons listed above we often gravitate toward using them, but they aren't without their problems.

Let's take an easy example. Using verbal or written instructions, teach a group of children how to make their first peanut butter and jelly sandwich. How complicated could that be? Let's pretend you started by giving each of them a box containing everything they'd need. Go ahead, after all it's only a peanut butter and jelly sandwich.

If you're like me, you came up with something like, "Place the box on a table, tape side up. Open the box. Take everything out of the box. Spread two spoonfuls of peanut butter onto a slice of bread. Then spread two spoonfuls of jelly onto a second slice of bread. Put both slices together. Eat."

Pretty simple, right? Well if we assume the children we are instructing have had past experience with those ingredients, other sandwiches and culinary tasks, so they can transfer that previous training to this application, yes. Or if we have prepared this learning with many lessons defining and describing the ingredients and actions, yes. But if not, our instructions may pose more questions than answers and yield more blunders than successes. Why? Because in this case, as in any teaching, our success often rests with our ability to put ourselves in the shoes of our students, assuming they know nothing, and to prepare, label and explain each and every step along the way so it can be used for future learning.

So now let's try those directions again, assuming nothing: "Good morning, class. Today you are going to make your first peanut butter and jelly sandwich. Everything you need is in front of you in what is called a 'box.' Make sure the box is on your desk with the shiny clear stuff that sealed the box, called 'tape,' pointing up. Peel off that tape. Open the box completely by bending back the 'flaps,' or folds which closed the box. That will expose all of the items packed into the box. Next, take each of those items out of the box and place them on the desk, starting with the bag full of 'slices'—or cut pieces—of soft, white squares called 'bread,' then the glass jar of purple-colored stuff called 'jelly,' the jar of brown-colored 'peanut butter,' the flat round thing which is a 'plate,' the bright silver-colored metal tool that is sharp on one side and has a point at the end called a 'knife,' and finally the other silver-colored metal tool with no point we call a 'spoon.'

"Let's start with the plastic bag of bread. Start by holding the end of the bag that looks like a tail with one hand, while with the other hand you turn the twisted piece of metal in the direction which loosens it. Remember that if the piece of metal, called a 'twist tie' gets tighter you must turn it in the opposite direction. Once the twist tie comes off, reach into the bag and remove two slices of bread. After that is done, we must close the bag of bread by holding the end that looked like the tail in one hand as you turn the bottom of the bag around and around with the other hand. That will close the bag and create a small area of tightly crimped plastic bag for you to place the twist tie back onto by twisting it until tight.

"Pick up the jar of peanut butter, so that the top or 'lid' is pointing up. Holding the side of the jar of peanut butter near the bottom with one hand, grab the lid with the other hand. You can then open the jar by turning the lid so your hand spins counterclockwise, or in other words the opposite way the hands of a clock turn, while holding the bottom of the jar still. If the lid doesn't loosen, try turning the lid in the other direction."

Need I go on? Frustrating, isn't it, and at this point, after all that, we only have an open jar of peanut butter and two slices of bread lying somewhere. Didn't you find yourself getting more and more annoyed as you fought off the desire to say, "Forget it, just starve!"

You probably also found yourself thinking this is not realistic, for who would attempt teaching something like this without some preliminary training or preparatory foundation, and the ability to make some assumptions about previous knowledge or skill? Truth is, if you reread those directions, I made many such assumptions, such as an understanding of: desk, sandwich, shiny, clear, seal, up, completely, pointing, peel, open, bend, close, expose, back, items, packed, start, bag, all, full, pieces, cut, jar, the color purple, the color brown, flat, round, square, soft, bright, the color silver, the substance metal, tool, sharp, side, point, end, grab, plastic, full, hold, glass, tail, hand, other, turn, twist, loosen, tighten, opposite, off, into, remove, one, two, close, hold, direction, clock, bottom, around, small, area, tight, crimp, pick up, top, near and spin, let alone that they are breathing. It's amazing how often we make assumptions without even knowing it.

For us as teachers it's remembering that though *we* can do the task at hand with-our-eyes-closed-in-the-dark-hands-tied-together-while-solving-a-crossword-puzzle because we have done it so many times, for our students each facet of any task must be detailed and defined. The success of our verbal or written instructions depends upon our ability to itemize every step of the new action, adequately describe those steps and then correctly sequence those steps in the most efficient way. All the while we must remember the importance and expediency of labeling what students learn so it can be used again without explanation, readying them for learning with adequate preparatory material, and helping them to use their previous training by transferring what they already know or can do to new situations.

Though verbal or written instructions, those step-by-step directions, are usually the first tool we metaphorically grab when teaching—because they are so perfect for learning many tasks—they are often not the best tool for the job, as is obvious with our peanut butter and jelly sandwich example.

As to trial and error, though it is a phenomenal tool for learning some things where creativity is as important as correctness, for tasks like our sandwich, can't you just picture trial and error yielding more jelly on the ceiling than on the sandwich, and hands covered in "peanutty" goodness?

So for tasks such as our sandwich it's pretty clear how much easier it would be to use imitation. Simple modeling so often is the easiest, but more important, the more effective and faster tool.

Obviously, more often than not we will use all three techniques successively or simultaneously in our teaching, such as *demonstrating* how to use a microscope as we label the parts and sequence the step-by-step *instructions*. Or we may teach students the *directions* and rules for writing a poem with a certain rhyming scheme, then have them use *trial and error* to explore and master the undertaking.

Though rarely will only one of those three teaching approaches be used alone, examples such as our sandwich point out the importance of preparing material, not making incorrect assumptions, labeling, transfer of training, modeling and self discovery in education. So the next time we reach for those instructions, assuming they are the best tool for the job, we might want to remember how difficult, frustrating and time-consuming it was to give instructions for something as simple as a peanut butter and jelly sandwich to someone who doesn't know what one is. ▨

ANOTHER WAY

The good teacher teaches information, the excellent teacher teaches what students need to know, the great teacher teaches students why they need to know it, but the extraordinary teacher makes students want to learn it. Though we need to do all of those things, I think the last one — getting kids to want to learn — can pose our greatest challenge. We can illuminate, inspire and reward. We can praise, push and explain. But sometimes it still proves difficult, difficult indeed. At those times it can be tempting to flirt with giving up, deciding that simply teaching the material is good enough. Often though it comes down to our simply finding another way, a way that makes students want to learn even if they don't realize why. Let me share three stories that may help describe what I mean.

For many years the salmon canning industry struggled with meager sales especially when compared to those of canned tuna fish. They tried, seemingly in vain, to garner some of the remarkable success and market share of that popular staple of the kitchen. However, it seemed that people were so used to the mild whitish look of the canned tuna that when they opened a can of salmon and saw pink they were turned off. Every attempt to get people to buy canned salmon suffered from the fact that it was pink. Many consumers even thought the product must have started white, like tuna, turning pink while in the can, almost as if going bad. Many companies gave up on even trying to market it.

But then someone decided there had to be another way: there had to be a way to get the average person to want to buy canned salmon. The result was one company launching a marketing campaign with a new slogan on every can of their salmon. It was a campaign that almost single-handedly changed the industry and bolstered sales to new heights of success. What, you must be wondering, could have done that? What could have gotten people to completely change whether they would buy the pink product? What words could have changed the mindset of so many people? Ready? The new label read: "Premium Canned Salmon: *Guaranteed to Stay Pink In The Can.*"

Amazing isn't it? Those simple words got people to buy canned salmon. In one fell swoop many people went from uninterested in the can of pink fish to seeking out that brand because it *guaranteed* them it would stay pink in the can. Instantly the product went from reviled or ignored to prized and sought after, all because someone found another way to the goal of *getting people to do something*.

The next story begins at a museum. Though there were signs all around the building nicely asking people to "Refrain From Touching" the works of art, people just couldn't resist laying their grubby little hands on every piece of treasured sculpture or antique furniture. So the curators decided to put signs directly next to each piece of art stating clearly: "Do Not Touch." That too failed. Next they placed attendants around the facility to ask patrons not to touch the objects. As audacious as it sounds people still seemed to go out of their way to grope the art.

At the point where most people would have given up in defeat, succumbing to the fact that this could not be stopped, someone found another way. No more guards, no more hassling offenders, no more threatening customers. In fact the next day every sign around the building asking people to "Refrain From Touching" was removed. So too the "Do Not Touch" signs next to each object of art. What replaced them? What new threat could stop this behavior? What could get people to stop their previous actions? New signs were hung that simply read: "Warning: Toxic Chemical Preservatives Have Been Sprayed On All Objects. Seek Immediate Medical Attention If You Accidentally Touch Anything." Talk about finding another way! Instantly, a new solution solved an old problem: *getting people not to do something*.

The last story takes place in a middle school where some of the young women who attended the school, seemingly excited about their newfound use of makeup, thought a clever prank would be to "kiss" the bathroom mirrors after applying outrageous quantities of lipstick, leaving lipstick splotches all over each mirror. After every incident the administration threatened punishment and tried to scare the culprits with lengthy missives and lectures, all to no avail. It seemed that with each threat the problem grew and spread. It also seemed nothing could solve the problem, leaving the staff little choice but to remove the mirrors.

That was, until one day when the principal *found another way*, calling for a large group of young ladies most suspected of the offense to a meeting in one of the bathrooms adorned with lip prints. Also in attendance was the head custodian. "Ladies," the principal began, "this immature, foolish, ridiculous nonsense of kissing the mirrors has to stop." As you can imagine, those words were accompanied by much eye-rolling and smirking from those assembled. "In addition," she continued, "it takes so much time and effort for our custodians to clean each mirror. In fact, I'd like you to see just how hard it is for them to clean those mirrors every day." At that signal from the principal, the custodian took the dirtiest mop he could find and swished it around in the filthiest toilet for a few moments before slapping it up on the mirror with vigorous scrubbing motions. Almost as fast as all of the girls gasped, covered their mouths in pseudo-nausea and felt sick, the problem was solved.

So sometimes it's simply that we must find another way to get our students *to do* something we *want* them to do, or *not to do* something we *don't want* them to do. Either way the solution may rest with how creative we can be as teachers.

As Albert Einstein reminds us, "The significant problems we face cannot be solved at the same level of thinking we were at when we created them." Possibly, the significant solutions we seek for our students cannot be found when they are at the same level of thinking as they have been. The answer may lie in simply finding another way. Think about sushi for a moment. I figure it this way: if some creative marketing person could not only discover a way to get people to try eating raw fish, but want to do it and pay a premium for it, I can figure out a better way to teach my students to do—or not do—just about anything.

Finding a way to get young students to spend more time reading may give rise to the teacher *limiting* the amount of

time they are *allowed* to read, increasing that amount of time
gradually with great fanfare and celebration as the students
earn the privilege to read more. Now this does require
acting worthy of an Oscar, but remember, someone once
figured out a way to convince many people to pay for the
privilege of going to a gym to sweat!

Finding a way to get third graders to learn something
may be to let it slip that the fourth graders are currently
learning it. Warning people they may not be able to do
something may be the way to get them to work at doing it.
Allowing a class to "overhear" you tell a colleague about a
future pop quiz may just get students to learn certain material better than announcing it. Giving someone the freedom
to do something may be the fastest way to get them to stop
doing it.

Will these attempts always work? Surely not. Does thinking a different way require extra effort? Of course. Will we
always be able to outsmart students, use reverse psychology
or manipulate the situation the way we want? No. So why
try? Because what we do and those whom we are entrusted
to teach are *that* important. Would it be easier to continue
our usual course? Yes, but the next time you are in the market and pass the aisle with the canned salmon, or go to a
museum, remember that sometimes finding another way can
be the best way. ▨

A Bowl of What?

Let's try an experiment. A little test, if you will. Quickly read through the following directions: start by driving down Route 26 and after the third traffic light turn left, pass two houses and make a left at the stop sign. Drive until you see the pink elephant reading a newspaper and turn right at the next traffic light. After driving nine miles, turn right on Route 94, then left onto Route 91, then another right onto Route 93. After you pass the sixth driveway, make a left on Route 19.

Now close your eyes and think back to the paragraph. What do you remember? I'll bet you don't remember many of the route numbers or which way you were to have turned when you got to them. I bet you don't remember how many driveways you were to have passed or how many miles you were to have traveled before turning. But I bet you do remember one thing. That's right, the *pink elephant reading a newspaper.*

Let's try another one. Read this list as fast as you can: a basket of tomatoes, a bushel of carrots, a plate of beets, a box of cucumbers, a bag of strawberries, a bowl of dancing pickles, a container of oranges and a case of apples.

Recite the list. Which did you remember and which did you forget? If I had to guess, you remembered the bowl of dancing pickles and forgot much of the rest. But far more important, which one do you think most of our students would remember? Why did we remember the pink elephant or dancing pickles? Well probably because they were absurd, unusual, humorous or bizarre. I guess it's human nature for us to remember that which is different, makes us laugh or is unexpected. Though I guess on some level I've always known that, as a teacher its power became abundantly obvious to me on one specific day.

One spring semester I was teaching a class at the university. It was a very demanding course which required the students to learn an immense amount of material. After a couple of months it came time for the midterm exam. I warned the students to know all of the material we covered in class as well as the assigned readings from two books. So each of them set out to study and remember sizable quantities of information as well as how to use it. Two weeks later the students took the exam.

That evening I started to grade the twelve-page test taken by each of my thirty students. I started working my way through each of their answers, saddened by errors I had to correct, elated by responses that were precise. I had only gotten to page six of the first exam when I was hit with a most bizarre and disconcerting answer. In response to a question asking students for their opinions about a certain approach to solving a problem, one student responded, much to my horror, "It stinks." (In truth it was a bit nastier word which I'd rather not repeat here.) I couldn't believe it. I was left wondering why this young man would have given an answer that was so brusque and unprofessional. Why indeed.

After finishing his exam I moved on to the next one. As my eyes read that same question I gulped in disbelief as I read the same answer. Test after test, student after student, I read the same awful answer. Then it hit me. I realized why all of my students gave that answer. It was because I had said it. That's right, *I* had said it. In remembering back to the class when we discussed the topic, I could hear myself offering my opinion with those exact words for emphasis. I couldn't believe it: of all the answers they chose to remember, of all the times they had flawless recall of my precise statement, it had to be those words. But they did; every one of them.

Why? I guess the impact of hearing a college professor use those words was indeed memorable. My slip of the tongue strangely helped students remember the topic and use those less-than-perfect words as the launching point for their opinions. Do I wish I had found better words to express my thoughts? Yes. But then I am left to wonder if my students would have remembered the topic as well.

The answer to yet another question on this exam had me giggling in amazement. I had asked my students to describe how an egg carton could be used as a teaching tool, reflecting back to a discussion we had in class about a neat way of developing kinesthetic memory for a specific technique by holding an upside-down egg carton. Remembering the odd image of my holding an egg carton in class was enough for them to remember the idea. That made sense, but what got me was the extra bit of information they all added to the end of their answers: "Remember to tell students to bring in an *empty* egg carton."

Why did they add that bit of information? Because I told them a story about a teacher friend of mine who used this approach but regretted the day she forgot to tell her students the egg cartons they were to bring to school had to be empty. For my students, remembering my telling of the horror and disbelief of this teacher as she watched an entire dozen eggs dump onto the floor became unforgettable. The smashed yolks, broken shells and sticky mess were too vivid to forget.

Reflecting upon that exam and those specific answers made me stop and think. What can we do to make important information more memorable for our students? How can we present material so it is unforgettable? Surely every fact we teach can't be accompanied by a humorous anecdote, but what can we do to help our students remember that which is important? Whether it's using a funny mnemonic device, a catchy slogan, a joke, a story or some out-of-the-norm way of presenting the material, we can help make learning more enjoyable and, more important, memorable.

Maybe whether our students remember or not is more in our hands than we may think. Maybe the trick is to make what we want them to learn *unforgettable*, rather than simply ask them to *remember* it. Maybe a healthy dose of pink elephants reading newspapers or bowls of dancing pickles can be more powerful for our students than hours of memorizing. Just remember, the egg cartons are to be empty when students bring them to school!

"IT'S NICE TO BE NICE TO THE NICE"

I t was another one of those days that started at 4:45 in the morning, still pitch black outside when the taxi pulled up to my house to take me to the airport. Now traveling as often as I do, going to the airport at that hour doesn't usually bother me very much but on that particular morning I wasn't in much of a mood. Well truthfully I *was* in a mood, it just happened to be a bad one. You see, strange as it may sound, the night before I had arrived home at around midnight *from* the airport after another trip. That's right, figure in unpacking, repacking, breakfast and a shower and I had a grand total of about two and a half hours of sleep. Not that my lack of shuteye was a good excuse for being grumpy but it surely was the cause.

So I jumped in the taxi and headed off to the airport, sadly with my bad mood in tow. Though I hate to admit it, my surly attitude got the better of me. I heard myself being short with the driver but I just couldn't muster anything better than far-less-than-friendly. I wasn't trying to be mean but I simply could not seem to make myself get any nicer.

Then it happened. After several minutes of my kindly driver asking questions and making polite small talk and my responding in a manner best described as cranky, he said, "I can't tell you how wonderful it is to have such a nice customer this morning." As his words registered in my mind I almost looked around the cab wondering where that *other* customer he was talking about was sitting, for he surely could not have meant me. But he did mean me. Almost instantly my attitude changed. A smile came to my face as I thanked him. Kindness came to my voice as I said I was sure everyone was nice to him. It was as though he had flicked the switch in my mind to turn on a good mood.

I know this sounds simplistic, silly and like a scene from a mediocre feel-good movie, but it's true. My bad attitude vanished as *I made his statement true*. My surly disposition changed as I began living up to his compliment, making what might have started as a bit of a fib on his part become reality. I could not help but prove him right, not because I had to, but because I wanted to.

For the rest of the ride this kindhearted older gentleman regaled me with some pretty amazing stories of how nice some customers had been and some equally amazing stories of how cantankerous others had been. Then at one point in a story he paused, looking thoughtful, and said, "You know, it doesn't cost anything to be nice, right?" I chimed in with polite agreement, but the truth be known, his words rang in my head for the rest of the day. I could not stop mulling them over and over until I realized that not only was being nice free, it was contagious, disarming and uplifting.

As grumpy as I was, that sincerely kind cab driver's statement about my being nice made my lousy mood disappear, lifted my spirits, brightened my disposition and gently gave me little choice but to fulfill that prophecy. In short, his kind attitude was contagious and I caught it.

At that moment I was reminded of an episode of the television series M*A*S*H in which the commander of the mobile surgical hospital, Lt. Col. Henry Blake, had become smitten with Miss Nancy Sue Parker, a young lady half his age who came to visit the camp. The evening of her first day on the base ended with a trip to the Officer's Club for a nightcap. The scene began with two of the hospital's senior officers, Major Margaret Houlihan and Major Frank Burns—both of whom strongly disapproved of their commander's behavior—sitting at a table in the club as the colonel and his guest arrived. Realizing they would have to greet the young women, the two majors agreed they needed only to be polite, nothing more, or risk looking as though they condoned the colonel's actions.

As Col. Blake introduced the perky, adorably sweet young woman to the pair of majors, the young guest gleefully spoke of how nice everyone at the camp had been to her. At that moment, a bit smitten himself, a starry-eyed Major Burns—dead set on being as curt as possible—helplessly blurted out: "It's nice to be nice to the nice" in the cheeriest voice imaginable.

Doesn't that have to be one of the dumbest sentences ever spoken? But as silly as it sounds, as cutesy as it may be, it's also true. It really is nice to be nice to the nice. In fact I think it may be *more work* to be mean to someone who is being nice, *harder* to be grumpy in the face of someone being happy, and *near impossible* to stay sullen rather than to succumb to the joyous attitude of a happy person in your midst. Major Burns had little choice, for that young lady's happy and positive manner was simply too infectious to be ignored and too potent to be deflected.

Surely we all know just being around a happy person can't change our mood from sour to sweet, but it can make it much harder for us to sustain that bad mood. It's clearly naïve to believe that simply being nice to people who disagree with us can convince them to change their minds but it may at least make them hear us out. Without a doubt it's way too simplistic to think being nice to people who are angry with us will turn them into our best friends, but it could disarm them enough to allow us to mend fences or soothe wounds. Quite simply, it's difficult not to get caught up in a wave of kindness and likeability when it's right in front of you. As that young woman on $M*A*S*H$ changed the behavior and character of her would-be detractor, and that cab driver changed my mean-spirited mood on that way-too-early morning, as teachers we can just as surely help change the attitude of a peevish student, ingratiate ourselves to parents and administrators, or lift the disposition of an entire class of young people simply with our attitude.

I know this approach may seem a bit manipulative, but it works, and it does so in a most positive and uplifting way. I know there will be times that being nice to someone we are angry with will be difficult, but this might be the best course of action. I know there will be days when we just aren't in the mood to be nice; what then? Well strangely enough, on those days that we are a bit grumpy but still can muster the wherewithal to pull this off, guess whose mood is the first to turn upward? Our own. Guess who is the first beneficiary of a better disposition? We are. Because it's hard to be grouchy around someone who isn't, even if that some-one is us!

Is this always the best approach? No. Will it always work perfectly? No. But can being a positive force, helping lift people's moods with your very spirit, or being perceived as nice, be a bad thing? I figure it's like the wonderful joke about the physician who prescribes chicken soup to an old man suffering from the common cold. After hearing this recommendation the patient asks, "Are you sure this will help?" To which the doctor replies, "No, but it couldn't hurt!" So the next time you're confronted with surly, be cheerful, because it's nice to be nice to the nice. Try it; what do you have to lose?

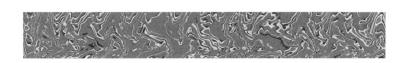

CREATIVITY

One morning many years ago, one of my children, sitting at the kitchen table looking very sleepy as he tried to wake up during breakfast before heading off to school, asked me, "Why do we have to go to school?" Surely every parent has heard that question, and just as surely you can bet I gave the perfunctory answer "Because," followed quickly with a diatribe about the virtues of learning as much as one can. But it got me thinking. Why *do* children need to go to school?

Of course we want them to learn information, gain skills, develop the ability to function as productive members of society, learn to communicate, think and feel. But of all that we can instill in our students, I believe creativity would have to be toward the top of the list. Being armed with information is important, but couple that with creativity and you can change a life. Possessing many skills is wonderful, but link those skills with creativity and you can change a community. Being able to communicate is vital, but combine that with creativity and you can change the world.

But what makes someone creative? Why do some people seem to be more creative than others? Is it remarkable intelligence or vast knowledge, so that only the smartest among us are destined to be the creative thinkers? Strangely, no. Conversely, often some of the most creative people on earth are of average intelligence. So if it's not intelligence, what makes someone creative? More important, how can we instill, teach and foster creative thinking in our classrooms? How can we help encourage the creative seed that rests inside all of us?

Though I have taken part in more than my fair share of group sessions designed to develop creativity through various exercises—and don't get me wrong, they were quite a lot of fun—they always left me invigorated to be creative, but unable to know how. How *does* someone act creatively? What do creative people do differently from noncreative people? What can I do to be more creative aside from simply trying to be so?

Then one day I found the answers I had been looking for in the pages of a wonderful book entitled *Cracking Creativity.* "Typically," writes author Michael Michalko, "we think reproductively, on the basis of similar problems encountered in the past. When confronted with problems, we fixate on something in our past that has worked before. We ask, 'What have I been taught in my life, education, or work that will solve this problem?' Then we analytically select the most promising approach based on past experiences, excluding all other approaches, and work in a clearly defined direction toward the solution of the problem."

After reading that passage for the first time, I thought, "So what's wrong with that?" That's what keeps us from putting our fingers in a light socket or touching a hot stove. That's how we know how to balance a checkbook or write a purchase order (well maybe not a purchase order, since I will go to my grave not understanding that mystery!). How could knowing what worked in the past so we can do it again be a bad thing?

Do you know what the problem with reproductive thinking is? It works! That's right, it works and because it works so well and is so ingrained in us, we use it all the time. Because of that, Michalko cautions, "Once we have an idea we think works, it becomes hard for us to consider alternative ideas." "Reproductive thinking leads us to the usual ideas and not to original ones."

In contrast, he goes on to say, creative geniuses think *productively*, revealing that "when confronted with a problem, they ask themselves how many different ways they can look at the problem, how they can rethink it, and how many different ways they can solve it, instead of asking how they have been taught to solve it." He continues, "With productive thinking, one generates as many alternative approaches as one can, considering the least as well as the most likely approaches. It is the willingness to explore all approaches that is important, even after one has found a promising one."

Basically, less creative people will stop looking for ideas once they think of a "good" one, whereas highly creative people continue to come up with ideas long after finding a good one, in the hopes of finding a great one. In short, we can never let the *good idea* become the enemy of finding the *great idea*.

In an amazingly illuminating example, Michalko writes that "Einstein was once asked what the difference was between him and the average person. He said that if you asked the average person to find a needle in a haystack, the person would stop when he or she found a needle. He, on the other hand, would tear through the entire haystack looking for all the possible needles."

To this end, creative individuals seem to use their imaginations less encumbered by strictures, patterns of thought, boundaries and entrenched notions. They are somehow better able to suspend associations from past experiences and remove predictability and logic from their thought processes, thus allowing themselves to think of many more ideas as well as wildly innovative and unusual possibilities. Along the way they question every aspect of what they "know to be true." In fact, as creative individuals, we are sometimes better served by great questions than by great answers.

Sadly, during the process of generating ideas, less creative individuals seem to be far more tempered by stereotypes, labels or past associations, often so focused on what they consciously or subconsciously believe to be obvious facts that they miss the hidden features, essential relationships or counterintuitive functions just off the beaten path.

For example, if I were to ask you to invent a sandwich, would your past associations limit your imagination to starting with two slices of white bread or would you have been creative enough to think of pulling out a loaf of raisin bread? Would you have been inventive enough to begin with two slices of French toast? Maybe, but would old associations have kept you starting your recipe with "take two slices of bread" even if you did test the creative waters of what kind of bread? Or would you have come up with a delicious recipe that uses breaded fried green tomato slices as the outside of the "sandwich," or two leaves of lettuce, or two sheets of edible paper?

This wonderful story by Bruce Vaughn illustrates how first "solutions" or "answers" can be as expedient as they are wrong. "There are two barbers in a small, isolated town. One barber's shop is littered with hair all over the floor. His own hair is a mess and he appears to be disorganized. The other barber's shop is clean and well organized. His hair is neat and looks nice. Which barber do you go to for a haircut?

"Working only from the information given above, you'd be wise to go to the unkempt barber with the messy shop. Being that the town is small and isolated, one can safely assume he gets his hair cut by the barber with the clean shop, whose shop is probably so organized because he doesn't get much business. Not to mention, his hair is neat and looks nice — probably the handiwork of the only other barber in town — the messy one."

It seems by simply thinking of what we see and hear — the *content* we perceive — in many and different *contexts*, we expand our creative palates. Looking at the same old event or information in varied and atypical ways can change its meaning, give new perspectives and become a catalyst for creative ideas.

It all comes down to this: if our knee-jerk response is always to do what worked before, how can we possibly ever come up with a better way? If we assume certain ways to be the best or only way of doing something or solving a problem, then every decision we make will be tainted by that assumption. In that way, as Stephen R. Covey so simply cautioned, often "the way we see the problem is the problem."

This way of thinking about creativity goes well beyond simple brainstorming or "thinking outside the box." True creativity, it seems, comes from forcing ourselves not to be prejudiced by our past successes as well as our failures. It demands a willingness and desire to think of many answers to a problem and worry about their validity or usefulness later. It warrants the perspective that sometimes large solutions may be the result of many little creative steps rather than just one big imaginative answer. Thus realizing, as Bill Willcox wrote, "The only thing standing between one big creative idea and success is about a million small creative solutions."

Even if some of those ideas didn't work once before or were deemed impractical in the past, they may end up being useful now. "For example," as Jack Gillett and Gary Schnuckle quipped, "the wheel existed for a long time in millstones before man used it for transportation. Why was that? There were no roads. But, inevitably, nice flat surfaces were invented, leading to wheeled vehicles. If your idea is way out, keep going, keep pushing. In doing so, perhaps you'll invent roads for your wheels." Or as James Russell Lowell put it, "Creativity is not the finding of a thing, but the making something out of it when it is found."

So I guess when we are filling out those purchase orders, the "same old way that worked before" may be the best bet, but when we are trying to set free our creative spirits, let us resolve not to grab the old familiar answers but reveal as many as we can, finding all those needles in all those haystacks. More important, let's resolve to help our students learn to do the same.

As teachers, what could be more important than helping every student discover the creative spark that resides within? In so doing, we gently place in the hands of all those whom we teach the ability and responsibility for the power of learning, that wonder and beauty expressed through creative minds, hearts and souls.

DWELLING ON DREAMS

"It does not do to dwell on dreams and forget to live..." said Albus Dumbledore in J. K. Rowling's *Harry Potter and the Sorcerer's Stone*. A wise man, that Dumbledore. Truer words could not be spoken for just about everything in life, but for us as teachers, that quite possibly represents the hardest balancing act of our profession. If you think about it, it is almost schizophrenic. On one hand, we want our students to enjoy their accomplishments and take pleasure in the success of the moment. We know the value of having them review what they have learned and enjoy the fruits of their labor.

On the other hand, we have a constant desire to push them to higher and higher levels of accomplishment. Then we become so worried about getting them to the goal, we forget — and we allow them to forget — to enjoy the process. The enjoyment of the steps along the way, the beauty along the path they take to their accomplishments, is lost to the goal of getting there. We spend so much effort "dreaming" of future accomplishments for our students that we forget to "live" and enjoy each moment.

But on the third hand, isn't a central part of our mission to help our students achieve higher and higher levels of accomplishment? If so, every moment counts. We can't spend time smelling flowers along the way; we have to get to the top of the mountain.

Still, on the fourth hand, we know that our students' time with us must be enjoyable. There certainly has to be hard work at times, but we can never allow it to become debilitating. Too much of that and we know we will lose them—in every way.

This reminds me of a dining experience I had years ago at a very fancy restaurant. About six of us were invited to go to dinner with a local celebrity who owned the establishment. This gentleman was obviously respected by his employees who did everything, and I mean everything, to make us feel pampered. As we sat down, the staff started bringing food to us as if for a State Dinner: course after course after course. It became obvious this was to be a wonderful experience. It also became obvious that each of us had our own waiter or waitress. Really! It was amazing. I felt like a king.

So what does that story have to do with the teacher's balancing act referenced above? Well, the servers drove us crazy. In an effort to be ever vigilant, on top of things, and to make us feel cared for, they were taking away our plates as the forks brought the last bites to our mouths. Actually, very often they took the plate if they *sensed* we had stopped eating for a second, even if the plate was still full. Of course no one said anything, not wanting to offend our host, but it drove us all nuts. The sense of frustration was overwhelming. A delightful plate of some beautiful creation was placed in front of us. We were told to savor it. Then, before we could swallow, it was taken away. I was never given the chance to enjoy the moment, because the staff wanted us to complete as many courses as was possible. In their minds, we *had* to finish the meal — every single course. A wonderful goal, but it left each of us frustrated.

I guess the bottom line is that we can never lose our desire to push our students further, but it must be managed so perspective is also never lost. That is what it's all about. We must keep sight of the goal and constantly encourage growth, but never allow it to loom so greatly as to be daunting. That goal can never overshadow the enjoyment of learning or the joy of what has been learned. Perspective, though, is a funny thing: it seems so obvious and logical, until tested.

We know our students' well-being is what is truly important. Whether they get to dessert or only get as far as the third appetizer, they must learn to taste every morsel along the way and enjoy it. They need to be proud of their efforts and abilities, all the while being reminded of the amazing things still ahead of them.

I think it comes down to helping students know that sometimes, as Dale Carnegie stated, "Success is getting what you want. Happiness is wanting what you get." We must help students balance *both* of those. It is a balancing act which is the responsibility of every teacher. When I get impatient, as often happens, I remember the following words of wisdom:

A Child
is a butterfly in the wind…
Some can fly higher than others
But each one flies the best that it can!
Why compare one against the other?
Each one is different…
Each one is special…
Each one is beautiful….

Those words help keep me on the path I want for my students. They help keep me on the path I want for *myself*. In their awesome power is the truth of our mission:

A hundred years from now…
it will not matter what my bank account
was, the sort of house I lived in, or the kind
of car I drove…
…but the world may be different because I
was important in the life of a child.

"*MOTIDISPIRATION*":
MOTIVATION,
DISCIPLINE AND
INSPIRATION

M otivation, Discipline and Inspiration. I wonder if any three words have been used more in the history of education. Some people think of them as separate concepts, while others believe they are related. I, however, don't just think they are related, I think they are one and the same; three sides, if you will, of the same coin. So I decided we needed a new word to describe that view, hence *motidispiration*: a blend of motivation, discipline and inspiration. Let me explain.

A great concern for some teachers is controlling a classroom full of students, thereby creating a disciplined environment. For other teachers, however, it is not a worry at all. They seem to do it naturally.

It doesn't matter which of those two we are, because motidispiration is the key, not only to creating a disciplined environment, but to getting to the next level. No matter where our students are now, motidispiration is the path to ever-greater heights. Whether it's taking students from weak to better, or excellent to brilliant, motidispiration is the key that unlocks the door every student must walk through. Simply, I define motidispiration as *progress or growth through controlled training, then teaching, to inspire students to be more motivated*. I like to think of it as the "Motidispiration Cycle," a six-part design for infusing inspiration and causing motivation, thus lessening the need for discipline.

Discipline: a word that nowadays seems synonymous with bad. A word that at once can make students grimace while putting a knot in the stomach of each of their teachers. A word that can just ruin a teacher's class, let alone day. But it shouldn't. It *can* be a good word and an even better concept. The trick is to differentiate between two types of discipline.

Reactive discipline is the one with the terrible reputation, and deservedly so. It is bad, always bad. It is putting out the fires of poor behavior after they have started to burn. It is reacting to bad behavior, placing the teacher in the position of trying to "catch up" to those behaviors, leaving little time or energy for moving the group *along* the path of learning, because we spend so much of it just keeping them *on* that path.

Proactive discipline, however, is good. It is positive and necessary. It is how we control and focus our students so they want to move, let alone have no choice but to move, along that path. Proactive discipline is how we determine outcomes, set the stride, control the classroom. Surely we will encounter, and must be capable of handling, both types of discipline. In fact, the skills and techniques used to manage and deal with both types of discipline are identical; it is only the context that differentiates them.

The Motidispiration Cycle

Control Them. This is where we create that controlled environment, the precursor to success which will move our students along the path to motivation. We must harness them, quiet and settle them, get them to be still, stop their fidgeting, focus their attention on us. This is where we get them to muster their intensity and concentration in anticipation of hard work.

Many years ago I watched an interview with the principal of an elementary school who in precious few years had taken the school's test scores and truancy rates from one of the worst to one of the best in that city. When asked her secret, this very passionate woman looked at her interviewer and in an almost scoldingly solemn way declared, "Learning cannot exist in chaos." How true. Learning, let alone growth, security, confidence and expression cannot flourish in educational chaos.

Nowhere is this described better than in *The Seven Mysteries of Life* by Guy Murchie. He illustrates with profound wisdom and insight what we, as teachers, know to be so very true when he wrote, "If a violin string is lying on a table loose and detached from any violin, some might suppose it 'free' because it is unconstrained. But what, one should ask oneself, is it 'free' to do or be? Certainly it cannot vibrate with beautiful music in such a condition of limpness. Yet if you just fasten one end of it to the tailpiece of the violin and the other to a peg in the scroll, then tighten it to its allotted pitch, you have rendered it free to play. And you might say that spiritually the string has been liberated by being tied tightly at both ends. For this is one of the great paradoxes of the world to be seen and tested on every side: the principle of emancipation by discipline."

Every time I read that passage I am reminded of its truth. We render our students free to learn and express themselves through the control necessary for a classroom full of children to function. We make it possible for them to communicate with each other and with us. But equally important is how that control *frees us*. For who truly can teach in an environment of chaos? Controlling them allows us to be the teacher we want to be, to teach what we need to teach, to explain, to emote, to enjoy, to savor, to grow. Released by that very control from the bondage of worry, anger and disappointment, we can enjoy our teaching and our students. To foster that environment, we can use the discipline techniques which follow to allow us to…

Train Them. This is where we train our students how to act, what to do and when, what is acceptable behavior and what is not. Notice I did not use the word *teach*. Much like training a pet, we need to instill in them actions and behaviors we want, and dissuade those we do not want. We can't assume our students know not to talk in class, that they need to have a calculator, use protective eyewear, not interrupt other students or take notes when we lecture. All of those actions, and many more, need to be trained. When "Fido" was a puppy, we didn't assume he knew not to chew every slipper in our home. No, we trained him not to. We kindly, lovingly, dispassionately, methodically trained him. We need do the same for our students (well, not the slippers, but most everything else). That will allow us to...

Teach Them. Now controlled and trained, we can teach students what to do to improve, offering specific techniques, concepts and information for their collective and individual growth and progress. We are free to truly teach, unhampered by disruptive behaviors that can otherwise bog us down. That will allow us to...

Inspire Them. We must be intense, enthusiastic and show we are as dedicated to them as we are to our subject. We must teach them how to get to the goal; but of greater value, we must explain the goal *and* its virtues. We have to convince them to try, ever improve, sense progress, never settle, feel emotions and find beauty all around them. How? Well, I think we do it by reveling in every success, no matter how small. It doesn't matter what or how little, just that it is successfully learned, giving us the opportunity to praise them and share moments of sheer joy. That will allow *them* to...

Motivate Themselves. Interesting isn't it? Did you notice this is the first time I said *them* rather than *us*? That's right, because we can't motivate anyone. The word "motivate" comes from the Latin "motum," which means "to move." If you think of it in terms of my wanting to move you from one place to another, I can only do that if I shove you or pick you up and carry you. And we all know how educationally unsound and ineffective, let alone damaging, that can be. We cannot motivate someone else; what we can do is inspire them to be motivated, *to move* themselves. In that way, we are living the words of William Butler Yeats who so perfectly reminds us, "Education is not the filling of a pail, but the lighting of a fire."

Certainly we hope that fire will come from within the student, and eventually it will, but sometimes a few sparks of enticement can help light the fire we seek. Extrinsic motivation, rewards our students earn for good behavior or positive growth, often serves to encourage and stimulate that conduct. It can be non-related extrinsic motivation, such as candy for learning an exercise, pizza for a successful class project, extra credit for having a pencil, or a gold star for a lesson done well. It can also be related extrinsic motivation, such as getting to have class outside on the first spring day, having their photographs posted for being selected students of the week, getting to go to a museum, having a guest speaker come in, or getting to do an activity they love. The problem with extrinsic motivation, as we all know, is too much of it for too long a time can lead to the "candy" being the only reason for the action.

So we need to wean them from, or at least reduce, extrinsic motivation, moving them over time toward intrinsic motivation: the self-driven desire to experience, excel and aspire because of how it makes *them* feel, the joy they receive, and their personal revelations of wisdom and the power of learning. Simply put, because *they want to*.

We need to get our students addicted to success. Even if at first it is progress made through the lure of extrinsic motivation, by experiencing success — technically or emotionally — those accomplishments generate the desire to do more. Yes, that may begin from a desire for more reward, but eventually the feelings of growth, progress and accomplishment will be the catalyst for even more of the same. And when that happens, we will remove or at least lessen the number of...

Discipline Problems. I think worrying about discipline problems is incorrect. It is like locking the gate after the horses have run away, like prescribing antibiotics after the patient has died. It is an autopsy. It may be the first line of defense, but it is the *last line* of offense. What made the student misbehave has not been attended to. Those problems are the result of a lack of motivation. We need to be *proactive* to remove the causes of poor behavior, but, more important, to *cause* good behavior. Our energies, therefore, should be used to inspire motivation. For if I am motivated to move myself, why would I be a discipline problem? Success or progress comes through inspiration and motivation, thus removing much of the potential for poor behavior and consequently the need for discipline.

Why Do Kids Misbehave?

Why *do* kids act badly? What would take an otherwise normal young person and make him or her be disruptive or troublesome? As oversimplified as it may sound, I think it all comes down to one reason: to get attention. We all want attention, and if we can't or don't get it when we behave, we're going to get it when we misbehave. That attention may come from the teacher in the form of a reprimand or from our classmates in the form of laughter. Either way, poor behavior gets rewarded. Why? Because of a simple fact of life: we'd all rather be *praised* than *punished*, but we'd all rather be *punished* than *ignored*. It could be that we are bored, frustrated or starving for recognition; we are going to act out to get that attention. One way or the other, we *will* get noticed.

Causes of Poor Behavior

So often, *we* cause the very behaviors we detest. Well, maybe we don't cause them, but we surely *facilitate* them. Combine our students' need for attention with certain things we do — or don't do — in classes and sometimes the results can be dreadful. If we recognize the specific catalysts or causes of bad behavior which follow, simply removing them, changing them or doing the opposite action may go a long way toward remedying the situation.

Poorly Paced Classes. I love a very fast paced class. I figure it helps keep people awake, though some of the best teachers I know have a slow pace. When the pace gets too slow, however, the result can be disastrous, as can slow, boring speech patterns.

"Down time" is so often when kids get into trouble, misbehaving if they don't have something better to do. Down time that occurs while we move between topics or activities must be eliminated so students stay focused on the work at hand. Long lectures can also create down time. Without question, some concepts and stories need time, but often we go on for minutes with what could be said in three words. And "minutes" are plenty of time to get a spit ball loaded, aimed and fired!

Another cause of down time is spending too much time with one person or small group of students while others grow restless. We can guard against this, but sometimes it may be necessary. In those cases, *time on task* is the key. While working with one group of students give a specific task to the other students that they can do themselves. Then, after finishing with the small group, query the others about their task.

Poorly Planned Classes. We need to keep students on task, to keep them busy not with the quantity of what we have them do, but by the quality of what we have them do. For that to happen, we must have a clear agenda, a detailed course of action, and a well-thought-out lesson plan, all rooted in our preparation: knowing the material cold. As "location, location, location" is for great real estate, "preparation, preparation, preparation" is for a great class.

Problems also occur when we don't take into consideration attention span. Imogene Hilyard said, "A child's chronological age in years is equal to his or her attention span in minutes." Having worked with college students for all these years, I question whether she meant seconds, but in either case, it is so true. Think about it: a ninth grader has about fourteen minutes. Use it wisely. That is not to say after the first fourteen minutes of class they will shut down, but rather they have fourteen minutes of intense concentration they can give you during a class. The trick is for us to spread those minutes throughout the class period, interspersing moments of review or lighter work so as to have the entire class period be fruitful and productive.

Too Much Routine. Though we need some routine for structure, too much can be deadly. When on autopilot, doing the same old routine they have down pat, our students can easily mess around. Variety is not only the spice of life, it can also make all the difference in the world when it comes to classroom management.

Unfocused Start of Class. The cause of many classes being unfocused is the way they start. A class that begins quickly, calmly and in a focused and controlled manner usually stays that way. Conversely, classes that start in a sloppy and rambunctious manner never seem to gain focus. Most of the problem comes from the making of announcements, signing of forms, collecting of papers and the endless conversations students "have to have" at that moment about anything and everything. All the while, other students slip into a fidgety, distracted state.

I advocate *training* students so none of those things occur at the beginning of class. Students are to come in, get themselves ready, focus on the work at hand, but they are *not* to come near me. With no gaggle of students pecking at me, I am free to think, greet my students and demonstrate through my own focus what is expected. They can speak to me from their seats with pleasantries or talk about an interesting topic, but nothing else. The only exceptions are for illness. Other than that, everything else must wait for the end of class.

You may be thinking, *"Five minutes* of announcements, questions and forms is *five minutes.* What does it matter whether it's the first or last five minutes of the class?" It matters a lot. Psychologically and sociologically it makes all the difference in the world, not just for those five minutes, but how those five minutes impact the prevailing attitude of the entire class. It is as healthy and liberating for the students as it is for their teacher.

Failure to Specify Rules. Students must know our expectations from the very first day they are with us. We can't wait until students break the rules to explain the rules to them. If we fail to clearly specify our classroom rules and procedures, how can our students be expected to follow them? We can't assume students know them and we can't explain the rules as they are being broken.

Lack of Readiness. Little we do can be as frustrating and debilitating for our students, thus creating an invitation for poor behavior, as asking them to do something for which they lack the mental, physical or emotional readiness to succeed. It always ends badly when our students don't have the mental readiness to understand the work at hand, the physical readiness for technical demands far ahead of their means or the emotional readiness for discussions of content beyond their grasp. Certainly we need to mentally, physically and emotionally challenge and stretch our students. But when that mark is well overshot, many of our students will, at best, tune out or be stymied, while others will have the perfect reason to misbehave.

Missing Tools for Success. Little could be more important for student achievement and our control of the classroom than sequencing *what* is to be learned, laying the ground work for progress and growth. If we have not previously taught our students the concepts, techniques and material now needed to succeed, they will not have the tools for that success. Students will then be doomed to fail and be frustrated, often acting out negatively on those feelings.

Unable to Communicate. If a student can't see the teacher due to obstacles which hinder direct sight lines, or can't hear the teacher who uses too soft a voice, he or she will become frustrated or give up altogether. We get the same result when students "can't understand" what we want because our directions or instructions are unclear. If they don't understand us, let alone can't see or hear us, we won't be able to communicate with them, engage them in class or keep them on task.

Getting Too Chummy. We as teachers all want our students to like us. But if we let them think of us as friends, or hesitate to discipline them because we want to be nice in order that they like us, we invite disaster. Yes, we want them to like us, but far more important is for them to *respect* us. As Ron Clark so rightly asserted, "You can't discipline kids and not love them, and you can't love them and not discipline them. The two must go hand in hand."

A Time Bomb Ready to Explode. Ignoring a problem rarely makes it go away. But because disciplining is as debilitating, energy sapping and unpleasant for us as it is for our students, we often ignore poor behavior. Then, after not reacting to that behavior, when we can't take it anymore, we explode like unstable dynamite, often *overreacting* to the behavior. Not only is that building up of anger as unhealthy as it is uncomfortable *for us*, the subsequent blowing up usually ends with our saying much we later regret.

But the worst part of this pattern of behavior is it trains students that they can get away with the poor behavior several times before they will be challenged. If you're starving and know you will get smacked on the hand only after the third or fourth time you get caught with your hand in the cookie jar, you're going to grab for the cookies. It's just in this case our students may be starving for *attention* rather than *food*.

Established Consequences. You know what I mean: those prescribed consequences or punishment for misbehaving, such as, "Students who forget their textbooks will write a one page essay on why students should not forget their textbooks." I don't like students being armed with that much information—information they then can use to make a reasonably informed decision as to whether doing a bad behavior is worth it or not.

I just don't want my students equipped with those facts. A little mystery in their lives can be good. If a student knows that clandestinely writing-in naughty words on another student's essay will result only in a detention, they may decide it's worth it to see that show. That's way too much information in my opinion.

Our Attitude. Have you ever gotten a chip on your shoulder which started a negative chain reaction of attitudes? I have, and I always regret it. A student behaves badly, so we muster a nasty tone of voice and a firm reprimand, he gets worse, we get nastier, he then gets even worse and we get even nastier. And so it goes, an ever-deepening pit of negative attitudes, one feeding the other. It gets us nowhere. As the words of Buddha tell us, "Holding on to anger is like

grasping a hot coal with the intent of throwing it at someone else; you are the one getting burned."

That scenario precisely describes a situation I had many
years ago when I first started teaching. I had this student
whose attitude was awful from the day we met. In class he
was almost combative. We started that war of who could
have the worst attitude and it went on for weeks. After class
one day, I called him into my office with the purpose of
throwing him out of the class. Before I did, however, I asked
him why he behaved as he did. With as much anger as sadness in his voice, the young man went on to tell me about
his recent attempt at suicide.

I sat there speechless, now listening to him rather
than reprimanding him. Instantly, *my* attitude toward him
changed from aggressive to supportive, angry to worried,
antagonistic to caring. I went back to being a teacher. I
wanted to help him change his attitude and behavior so he
could experience joy, not only in my class, but in his life.
Now in classes when I have a student like that, I remember
to be a teacher first and live the words of Jesse Jackson who
warned, "Never look down on anyone unless you are helping them up."

It all comes down to one remarkable statement. Words
that are as true when we are being negative, discouraging
and disdainful as when we are being positive, encouraging and uplifting. Words by Dennis and Wendy Manner-
ing that are at the core of being a teacher: "Attitudes are
contagious. Are yours worth catching?" The answer to that
question — for us and our students — may be as important
as anything we teach.

Reinforcing Negative Behavior

Some of the most common responses to poor behavior take the form of *reinforcing negative behavior*. That's when poorly-behaved students get attention from you or other students for bad conduct. We catch them doing something wrong and then "reward" that action by letting them know they "got to us," or that they can derail our teaching. In that way, we prove they control the class by "pushing our buttons," and by so doing we *reinforce* that very behavior. What follows are the four most common ways we reinforce negative behaviors.

Shouting. Yelling only fuels the fire of an ever-escalating volume contest between teacher and students. We yell, they yell louder, so we yell still louder, and on it goes. And where it ends is always bad. It is antithetic to education, compassion and positive communication. It sidetracks real teaching, severely limits the manner in which the teacher speaks, and often ends up being the norm for classroom dialogue. Every time I hear a teacher yelling at his or her class I am reminded of the astoundingly astute words of Dagobert Runes: "You cannot train a horse with shouts and expect it to obey a whisper."

Threatening. We all know this is a lose-lose proposition, but it still rears its ugly head all too often. Making a threat to a misbehaving student is like waving a red flag in front of a bull; he has no choice but to "call us on it" just to test us. We have challenged him as if we had thrown down the proverbial gauntlet. Then we have either to make good on our threat, which is all too often something we regret having threatened, or back down and look powerless. Usually the student wins: game, set and match.

Fear and Sarcasm. Many of us lived through the days when this was the way it was done. A teacher ruled by fear and sarcasm. Fortunately, those days are gone. When used, fear and sarcasm only serve to let our students know they "got to us": wrecking our mood, ruining our flow, interrupting our teaching, and hijacking our classes.

Punishment. I'm not a big believer in punishment. Do I use it? Yes, but I hate it because it proves to me that *I* failed: I had to resort to punishment because I couldn't find positive ways to solve the problem earlier. I let it become this bad. I didn't take positive steps to improve the situation, so now I am left with few choices. If I had just taken the "daily vitamins" of proactivity, I may have prevented the "disease" of bad behavior now confronting me.

All I know is if we use punishment, it must be done sparingly, carefully and dispassionately. The reason I dislike punishment stems from the fact that punishment may make students *stop the bad behavior*, but it won't make them *want to do the good behavior*.

If you feel you have dug yourself into a hole with these negative approaches, I would go with the advice of Molly Ivins who said, "The first rule of holes: When you're in one, stop digging." Yelling, threatening, sarcasm and punishment often just dig a deeper hole. Benjamin Hoff, when describing the Wu Wei principle of Tai Chi in his wonderful book,

The Tao of Pooh, illustrates the problem as well as its solution when he writes, "The Wu Wei principle underlying Tai Chi can be understood by striking at a piece of cork floating in water. The harder you hit it, the more it yields; the more it yields, the harder it bounces back. Without expending any energy, the cork can easily wear you out. So, Wu Wei overcomes force by neutralizing its power, rather than by adding to the conflict. With other approaches, you fight fire with fire, but with Wu Wei, you fight fire with water."

We must remove the causes of poor behavior, not fight them. We must offer reasons for students to behave, as well as penalties when they don't. We must instill in them the desire to be part of the progress of the class, not to be its impediment. We must remember it is far more productive to reward the good than to punish the bad. Even if our negative reactions do work, their effects are short-lived and usually foster negative feelings of hate, anger and embarrassment rather than positive feelings of cooperation, inspiration and striving for growth. So often, after a student has been dealt with negatively, I am left thinking, "Well, if he wasn't a real discipline problem before, he sure will be now!" So if at first we don't succeed, let's find a different way.

Proactive Techniques and Approaches

What follows are proactive techniques and approaches — more positive ways — for controlling and disciplining students, improving behavior in classes and inspiring motivation.

Reinforcing Positive Behavior. If it's true all we want is praise, encouragement, recognition — that "pat on the back" for success and completion, or trying and making progress—there is really only one path to take. The only approach to discipline that is long-term, long-lasting, self-disciplining, proactive, transferable, positively stimulating and uplifting is *reinforcing positive behavior*. Basically, catching students doing something good, praising those positive, wanted behaviors and desired actions, thereby causing an increase in the good behaviors, no matter what they may be. It's simple: "If one person can say something to make someone feel bad, then maybe another person can say something to make him feel good." Praise encourages good behavior by making the student feel the benefits and rewards of *that* behavior. Reinforcing positive behavior keeps well-behaved kids behaving well, and makes poorly behaved kids behave better.

If needed, I'll "rig" events or stretch the truth a bit to creatively manufacture situations in order that students experience positive attention, so they taste the praise they've craved all along. But most important, we must remember to praise approximation: to applaud the steps along the way to the goal, no matter how small they may be.

Some say too much praise is a bad thing. Let me ask you a question: do you ever get tired of hearing compliments about how good a teacher you are? Probably not. Now, if the praise is insincere, "over the top," ridiculously lavish or given when not deserved, the purpose and power of the praise is diluted. But small doses of subtle recognition are all that is needed: a "thumbs up," a smile, a nod of the head, an okay sign or a few words of praise.

That said, care does need to be given with older students, especially those of high school age. Though praise for groups of students or the entire class is perfectly fine, we do need to guard against praise which is too overt, or too much praise for single individuals, so they don't get branded a teacher's pet. Again, judicious care, subtlety and spreading the wealth of positive comments around the class may remove any problem.

The Never-Ending Circle of Growth. Whatever the opposite of a vicious circle is, this is it. To me, it represents teaching at its best: linking reinforcement of positive behaviors to constructive criticism. It is best summed up in the words of former President Dwight D. Eisenhower when he defined leadership as "the art of getting someone else to do something you want done because he wants to do it." This is where we praise, and thus reinforce, something a student is doing well to reward her success and bolster her self-esteem. Then immediately follow with one bit of constructive criticism which identifies something that needs improvement, offering specific comments on what to do to improve. Students feed on the positive comment, but at the same time know what to do to improve.

With comments such as, "Nancy, your printing is beautiful; now let's remember to keep within the margins," the never-ending circle of growth begins. The trick is for the little person on your shoulder — you know, the miniature you that sits there and serves as your eyes, ears, conscience, guide and filter — to go to work. His or her job now, while you are busy teaching the class, is to stare at Nancy, just waiting for her to stay within the margins so you can praise that success and offer new constructive criticism. The little man or woman on your shoulder remembers so you can offer reinforcement at the first sign of improvement. With each pass of the circle, each nod of our praise and suggestion for improvement, we foster growth which is as uplifting as it is successful.

It does take an enormous amount of time to support every single student in this way. And though we can sometimes "get them" in groups, or as a whole class, often it is done one student at a time. But getting, converting and keeping every student on the right path is worth every minute.

Your Personality. Have you ever stood in the customer service line at a store waiting to return a product that was a few days past the "return by" date? Watching the clerks assist each customer ahead of you, didn't you pick out the one who seemed the easiest mark and secretly hope you got him? Didn't you decide the person at counter number one was someone you wouldn't want to cross but the person at counter number eight seemed a soft touch? Well, students who are bent on misbehaving to get attention make those same decisions. We each need to develop a personality they won't want to cross or challenge, a personality so strong and intense they decide it's just not worth "messing with" or "trying" you. Sad to say, but in their minds an easier mark may be found in the next class.

Draw Them In. The more positive goal of the previous entry is to use that intense persona — that *power of personality* — to capture the hearts and minds of our students. Through that ability, we can focus their energy, strengthen their concentration and empower their resolve. Call it mesmerizing, evangelical, enthralling or charismatic; it can be the means by which we control any classroom.

Start Firm. When I first started teaching, it was suggested to me that I begin every class firmly to settle the group, then once all is going well, relax the reins as the period goes on. Certainly, that isn't the only way, but it surely does seem to be the most secure and reliable way. We can always loosen our control, but it's very difficult for many to tighten it. The same advice holds true on a grand scale for the entire school year. I'm not talking about Dr. Jekyll morphing into Mr. Hyde but just a bit firmer start can make a huge difference.

Be Consistent. Essential to achieving a controlled environment is a teacher who is consistent from student to student and day to day. We must be consistent when dealing with our "best" students or our "far-from-best" students, when we are in a good mood or in a bad mood, and when confronted by the same behavior from different people. Consistency breeds standards and expectations; inconsistency breeds contempt.

Act Not React. When a teacher is confronted with a behavior problem, *reacting* to the situation — that knee-jerk response — almost always ends badly, reminding me of the prophetic words of Publius Syrus: "I have often regretted my speech, never my silence."

Taking a moment to think, then calmly *acting* upon that same situation, however, leads to a concerted, reasoned, thought-out, dispassionate response. That course of action almost always ends well. We just need to remember the words of the Chinese proverb: "If you are patient in one moment of anger, you will escape a hundred days of sorrow." How many times in my life have I remembered those words ten minutes *too late* and lived to regret it?

Defuse First. Figuring out what caused a discipline problem is important, but as it is happening, it is far more important to defuse or stop it in its tracks. Analysis of what happened, thoughts of who was culpable and reflection about what *we* could have done better — more proactively — to prevent the problem, need to wait. We must put out the fire, then figure out what happened.

Show Interest. Showing interest and concern — making it a point to say something positive to every student as often as possible — is one of the most proactive ways to inspire them. Even a simple "How's everything?" or "Great job in class today!" as you pass them in the hall is good. Even better is when we can say something more personal, especially about their interests outside of class, such as, "How's your cold?" or "How was your baseball game?" To that end, at the start of the year, have students fill out information cards that include their interests. They can be incredibly helpful, especially for younger students.

It is difficult. It can challenge even the best memory of the most caring teacher. But it matters. Why? Because from a behavior standpoint, it's hard for students to be a "rat" to someone who takes an interest in them. And from the human standpoint, it matters so much in the life of a child, a life we make better with every passing word.

Balance. I often worry that I dwell on the negative. Think of it: much of our job is assessing errors, finding what's wrong and deciding what needs to be fixed. In some ways, we are professional nitpickers. It's not that we are pessimists, but rather sometimes we use so much energy and concentration finding problems that we forget to balance our thoughts and—even more—our comments. So, years ago, I promised myself I would try to say something positive for every negative. I don't always succeed, but it does help me to remember that every half-empty glass is also half full.

Use Necessary Repetition. Repetition is certainly part of what we do. I sometimes think clever, disguised ways of saying "let's do that again" make up a large part of a teacher's vocabulary. And though sometimes we could target our teaching to reduce the amount, frequent repetition is necessary for reviewing material that has been learned, practicing techniques, putting what's been isolated back in context, and reinforcing basic concepts.

I think we should use those necessary repetitions as opportunities to praise. Each repetition gives us the chance to reinforce positive behaviors in our stellar students so they don't get bored, and link reinforcement of positive behaviors to constructive criticism for those needing more dramatic improvement. Since we're going to repeat something anyway, why not make the most of it?

Notes Home. During my junior year in college, I was given a very large solo in a piece with the wind ensemble. Though the composition had many smaller solos, mine was quite daunting. I don't think I've ever worked harder on anything in my life. The night of the performance came. I guess the fates were with me and the planets aligned correctly; I played it pretty well. Or so I thought. During the applause at the end of the work, the conductor had every soloist stand but me. You could hear a hushed gasp from the ensemble as it became clear I was not to be recognized. I was devastated. I remember walking back to the dorms replaying my performance over and over, wondering what was so bad as to offend my conductor. I had no answer, but I felt terrible.

The next morning I arrived at school quite early, and as usual, checked my mailbox. There I found a letter from my conductor. He apologized profusely for forgetting to have me stand. He went on to explain that he was going to have all the other soloists rise, then have me stand at the end, but in his worry about not forgetting anyone, he forgot me. But of far greater significance, he wrote about being proud of my effort and accomplishment. Isn't that amazing? In the real scope of things, it was a stupid little solo. However, to him—a real teacher—it meant much more.

You know what? I still have that letter somewhere up in my attic, and though I can't really tell you what it said, I will never forget how it made me feel. Now, all these years later, I think of him every time I write a note to a student or parent. If you haven't done it, try it; you will become addicted to the smile each note brings and the growth it encourages. Though I prefer to write, because then I control the amount of time I spend, some like to use the telephone. Either way, simply receiving "good news" from school will shock students and parents as much as delight them. And *after* Mr. and Mrs. Jones receive your letter or phone call praising their daughter Sue for her great work in learning her times tables, the conversation at home will go something like this:

"Susan, get in here!"
"What?"
"We just got a letter from your math teacher."
"Oh no, did I kill someone?"
"No, it said something about your times tables, and that he was proud of you. And so are we."

Those are moments that can change and shape lives, last a lifetime and represent teaching at its best. And every time you send a note home about a student's progress, improvement or success you do far more than make someone's day: you help make someone's life. They *may* forget what you said, but I'm here to tell you, they will *never* forget how you made them feel.

So promise yourself to send three notes home this week, but realize you will get addicted. It will start with three, and then six, then ten and before you know it you'll be hooked; not to the writing, but to the faces of the students whose lives you affect. Remember, you promised.

Engage Them. A student who is truly engaged in a class is unlikely to behave poorly. However, if a student is not engaged in the process he will be idle, bored or frustrated. At best, he will not be learning; at worst, he will become the source of behavior problems. Neither is acceptable.

We need to communicate to our students not only the meaningful information of facts and knowledge, but equally meaningful comments of praise and constructive criticism.

Stop Discipline Cells. Thirty kids don't all decide to mis-behave at once. They just don't. It starts with one or two students in one spot and one or two in another spot. And then it spreads from there like a virus. The trick for us is to be so observant, sensitive and on top of what's happen-ing in our environment that we prevent discipline cells from forming, and stop those that do form the second they start—before they can spread to other students or get out of hand. No advice is better than Mike Leavitt's, "There is a time in the life of every problem when it is big enough to see, yet small enough to solve."

Nonverbal Discipline. When it comes to controlling students with words, less is good, none is better. We can't underestimate the power of nonverbal discipline. Just *standing in silence*, glaring at students who misbehave is far more potent and compelling than just about anything we can say. When we speak, all too often we diminish the power of our personality, and "let them win" by confirming they "got to us."

Though that unadorned stare is usually persuasive enough, we can add a simple shaking of the head from side to side as if saying "no," the pointing of an index finger with outstretched arm, or the walking over and standing in front of students who are disruptive. Simply offering a look of disappointment can also be very effective; sometimes, depending on the student, far better than a look of anger. Some years ago, after I looked at a student disappointedly, she said to me, "In the future, would you just yell at us? It's far easier to take than when you look disappointed." That taught me a lot.

A Person of Few Words. Though silence may work best to control disruptive students, when we do choose to speak, being a man or woman of few words is almost always better than being the author of a long-worded, passionate reprimand. Short, pointed, powerfully calm statements to students who are behaving poorly, such as "No," or "Not again," work extremely well.

Fear of the Unknown. Looking directly at a student and emotionlessly saying, "I wouldn't do that again if I were you," is an example of this. It is *not* making a threat, but rather allows a student's imagination to concoct possibilities far worse than any reality we would threaten. The worry of not knowing the "what" of the teacher's statement makes the alternative of behaving well a more appealingly certain outcome.

Be Schizophrenic. Though it may sound crazy (sorry, I couldn't resist the pun!), this is where we go from our normal, vivacious, enthusiastic self, to disciplining a student with something like a cold, silent stare or terse "not again." But then we jump back to teaching the class—on task and happy—even more excited, carefree and cheerful than before the interruption. Students come to understand they can't derail our plans, push our buttons or ruin our demeanor; quite frankly, it offers little reward and takes the purpose out of misbehaving.

Why?

What's this all about? What are we trying to inspire our students for? Is it really that important? You know the answers to those questions; all teachers do, that's why we are who and what we are. But I'd like to share a story with you that helped me come to understand it so much better. A few years ago I attended the spring concert of a former student of mine. At the end of the concert, as was the tradition at this high school, the seniors in the band came to the front of the stage to give their director a gift. It was a pole, a metal pole. All I could think was, "Nice gift?!"

But in the back of the crowd of seniors, I could see two students holding something large, wrapped in a blanket. After the puzzled audience — and band director — had a moment to digest the idea of a metal pole as a gift, those two students made their way to the front of the stage. With almost solemn dignity, they unveiled a sign. It was a metal street sign to be affixed to that pole and placed in front of the school. It was a sign for the reserved parking space they somehow finagled for their band director. Now I don't know about where you teach, but where I teach, a parking space is worth its weight in platinum.

Then the seniors spoke about their four years with the ensemble and their teacher. No one spoke of how many trophies they won, how many difficult pieces they performed, or the results achieved at any contest. Instead, they spoke of how their teacher and this ensemble changed their lives, helped them become better people, gave them eyes to see the beauty in the world, and made them able to feel emotions as they walked through life. That's what it's all about. That's why it's so important. Because our students, just like us, don't remember facts, they remember feelings. Not just from our telling them what to do, but by our inspiring them to do it.

How?

But how do we inspire? Well, I have a little formula: "I = C + P + E." "I," inspiration, equals "C," curiosity: for learning, for what's on the next mountaintop, for what's possible. Plus "P," praise: for the steps along the way, for beauty, for trying, for effort. Plus "E," emotion: for the chills, the tingles up the spine, the tears, the tapping into one's soul. That's inspiration.

I bet you're wondering why there was no mention of an "E" for enjoyment. I believe enjoyment is important, but I also believe it is a byproduct of being inspired through curiosity for what we can be, praise for what we are, and feeling the emotions of what we learn.

How do we inspire? A sentiment borrowed from Socrates says it best: Excite me and I will learn anything, make me curious and I will learn even more. Our enthusiasm must excite our students to be curious, to want to learn, to explore, to try, to follow, and to *learn* that *learning* itself is amazing. If our classes are controlled, we can train our students. Then teach them and inspire them. Then watch them motivate themselves, grow and flourish.

We will have given them the greatest gift imaginable: the appreciation of themselves and of life. We will have taught them to aspire, and to live the words: "Go as far as you can see, and when you get there, you'll see farther."

I'd like to ask you a question. If the moment you started reading this chapter I placed a small white box on a table in front of you with no words of explanation, would you, by the end of the chapter, be wondering what was in it? And as the minutes passed, if I kept turning and moving it around the table, would your wondering turn to puzzlement? If then I intermittently stuck flashing lights of different colors, shapes and sizes on the box to continually draw your attention to the box, would you become curious? When I present this chapter as a session for conferences that is exactly what I do.

At the end of the session, I simply put the box back in my briefcase with no words of explanation. Most often, that action is accompanied by an audible groan from all present, and quasi-angry questions about what was in the box. My answer is always the same: "Oh, the box. Are you *curious* about what's in the box? I think Socrates would have liked that!"

I then open the box, revealing nothing but a worthless, crumpled-up, empty candy wrapper. After people settle in to their disappointment, I look inside the wrapper, and show to all a brand new $100 bill. Then I remind them that things aren't always as they seem. It's not what our students are; it's what they can become. Every child must be taught to reach for the stars. Every child can learn and become anything, if *we* help them to bring it out.

No one taught me this better than my mother. You see, my mom was a wonderful artist, as talented as she was humble. She had a studio in the basement of our home, and on the wall next to her easel hung a very small frame which my dad made for her. In the frame was a small piece of paper onto which she copied the following words, elegantly adorning them with a flowering vine. They are from a letter of introduction from patron to pope which reads: "The bearer of these presents is Michelangelo, the sculptor. His nature is such that he requires to be drawn out by kindness and encouragement. But, if love be shown him and he is well treated, he will accomplish things that will make the whole world wonder."

Who knows what student, even those that may seem like crumpled-up candy wrappers, may, with love and encouragement, "...accomplish things that will make the whole world wonder"?

"How Do You Know?"

"There once was an old farmer who kept horses. One night, during a great storm, a section of his fence collapsed, and all eight of his horses escaped. The following morning, several members of the surrounding village came to offer their condolences. The old man asked, 'Why are you so sad?' and the villagers replied, 'You have lost all of your horses: this is a disaster!' To this the old man asked, 'How do you know?' The villagers walked away, shaking their heads in confusion.

"The next day, all eight horses returned, bringing with them twelve wild stallions. The villagers returned, exclaiming their joy for the old man's great fortune. The old man simply asked, 'Why are you so happy?' 'All of your horses have returned, and you now have many more! This is a good thing!' exclaimed the villagers. The old man again asked, 'How do you know?' and again the villagers left, dumbfounded.

"The following morning, the old man's son arose, and went out to tame the new, wild stallions. In so doing, he was thrown, his leg broken. The villagers returned, with great sadness on their faces. The old man immediately noticed this, and asked, 'What saddens you so?' The villagers replied,

'Your son has broken his leg! This is terrible!' Again the old man asked, 'How do you know?'

"Not two weeks had passed before the Emperor's men rode into the village. The war had greatly ravaged their front lines, and they sought fresh young blood to serve in their army. The old man's son, however, could not be drafted, for he had a broken leg. When the villagers heard about this, they said, 'How lucky! If he had been drafted he would almost certainly have died or suffered terrible injury.' The old man said, 'Is it lucky? How do you know?'"

Does that mean some good things can't be just plain old good, and it may be virtually impossible to find the good in some bad that befalls us? Sure. But that remarkable parable from Lao-Tzu, the father of Taoism, shows us how *our perspective* tempers our view of all that happens to us. *We decide* how we will characterize all we encounter. I know that may sound like optimism run amuck, but it's really more about being a realist.

Things are what they are. The situation I am in *is* the situation I am in. How am I going to perceive it, what can I learn from it, how can I grow from it, and what positive aspect or benefit can come from it? How's that for easier said than done? But what a wonderful gift we give our students when we help them to understand its truth; what a wonderful gift we give ourselves when we realize its power.

Picture the two of us sitting in a fancy restaurant having a cup of coffee after dinner. All of a sudden I knock my cup off the table, sending the fragile china vessel plummeting down to the floor. It shatters into a million pieces with a most violent crash. At that moment, as I sit there horrified and embarrassed, every single patron in the restaurant turns and looks at me. My first thought: "I can't believe all these people are staring at me thinking I am an idiot. They all just *had* to superciliously look at the moron who dropped his cup." I feel so bad.

But *I* am the one who decided to characterize those events that way. The reality of that scenario more likely was that those people suddenly turned and stared at me because they were startled by the loud crash. And human nature being what it is, they simply turned in my direction as a reaction. That's it — nothing more — nothing less. All of those bad feelings were manifested only in my imagination. The reality — the truth — was far simpler. It's all about perspective; how we see our reality, like George Carlin wrote, "Why is it the other side of the street always crosses the street when I do?" It's all in how we see it.

As well, can we always know what good lies in that which we view as bad? And will we necessarily ever be aware of *that good*? Perhaps not, but those virtues, like the ones that follow, may be hiding in the most unlikely places. Each is an opportunity for us to be the best teacher we can be.

Finding Strength

Devastating cuts are being proposed for your department. You are being called to meeting after meeting with administrators and are having to defend the value of what you teach.

As a result, parents have become motivated and mobilized to fight for what is right. And possibly even more important, you have strengthened your resolve to understand the value of what you do, commit to being an even more effective teacher, and cherish every opportunity to teach young people. Sometimes we find strength — inner and outer strength—in places where we would never think to look.

Growth Isn't Always a Climb Straight Up the Mountain

Steve, one of your best science students, a joy in every way, comes to you to find out the results of the state science fair competition. You have to tell him that he didn't make the finals despite the fact that he worked harder than he knew possible.

You seize the opportunity to explain how he must keep that one event in perspective, the reality of competition, that those results can't undermine his hard work and growth, and that sometimes the falls of life give us the motivation to climb even higher. Your encouragement at that moment helps him deal with that news, and with all the disappointments in his life, giving him the willingness to try harder after each of them.

Teaching Tools Which Last a Lifetime

Susan, a delightful young student in your class, could not remember the names of the days of the week. She tried but failed. You, her teacher, recognizing the problem, call her in for help and explain the use of a simple mnemonic device.

Many years later, fearing she would never pass a chemistry exam on the periodic table of elements, she remembered you and those days of the week. She passed the exam with flying colors, and once again you proved to her that she could learn anything.

Deal with Emotions

While discussing a magnificent poem with your high school English class, you pause to describe to the students how this emotional work was written in honor of the writer's father who had recently died. You ask them to pour their hearts into each word. You talk about the sadness of losing a loved one and the grief this work captures. Hard lessons, but lessons that need be taught. For the rest of the class you notice that Sarah, one of your students, is extremely overcome with tears. You quietly walk over and ask if she is okay. She nods for you to continue.

At the end of class you meet with her. Through the tears she proceeds to tell you that her father was just diagnosed with a disease that will soon take his life. You feel awful that you unknowingly put this child in a state of inconsolable emotional turmoil right there in what should be the safety of your classroom.

Months later, only days after her father's passing, Sarah comes to you. She thanks you for your concern and care, but far more significant, she thanks you for helping her learn how poetry can soothe the heart; how it can make the tears come and then dry them; and how it can offer a way of expressing her sorrow as well as the love she had for her father. She continues describing how that class, all those months ago, as overwhelming as it was, helped prepare her for the future.

Bolster Self-Esteem

Every day, Bill would come to baseball practice. Every day, he would barely get through practice without a disaster.

Every day, you would grow more and more frustrated at his lack of ability. Without a doubt, he was the weakest link in the chain that was your team. He was the anchor that weighed everyone down.

One day he came to you and said, "I know I'm a terrible baseball player, I should just quit. I stink." You found yourself in quite the bad situation. And though fleetingly you thought that might be the best thing for the team, you knew it wasn't what was best for him. As surely as you wondered whether Bill would ever play all that well, you knew he needed it in his life.

You had a long talk with Bill. You took the time to bolster his self-esteem, to convince him you valued his worth as a person just as much as his worth as a player, that every member contributes to the whole, and that as long as he worked as hard as he could, you would never give up on him.

Twenty years later, a young Bill, Jr. came home from school and asked his dad whether he should sign up to play baseball. The answer was a resounding "yes" as the dad regaled the boy with stories of his experiences. But what Bill, Sr. really was remembering was how special and important you made him feel at a time when he didn't feel very important. The fatherly support for his son playing baseball was as much about how you taught "the person" that was Bill as about how you taught "the player" that was Bill, and about the self-esteem you helped instill that has sustained him all his life.

A New Way of Thinking

Joan had been studying Spanish for two years, and though she had lovely inflection and a wonderful spoken vocabulary, her ability to read the language was extraordinarily weak. She just couldn't get it. You tried and tried but to no avail. Failure was at hand. She was ready to give up, and so were you.

But you didn't. Instead you started asking Joan's other teachers and guidance counselor if she was having difficulties in other subjects. Slowly a pattern emerged, until finally you realized she was having trouble processing any written material. You facilitated her getting help for a previously undiagnosed special need. Now, with the aid of professionals in that area, she was being helped to find new ways of learning that would work for her. Her life now had possibilities she never imagined.

Conclusion

Do our "bad" situations always turn out that rosy? Can we be sure those benefits appear even though they may arrive years after students leave our lives? Can "bad" situations turn even worse? Do our best efforts sometimes fail? The answers are obvious. But we are teachers, and we know the lessons learned in adversity can sometimes be the most powerful and life-changing of all. May the good in life follow you and your students closely. But when the bad comes, may you help those whom you teach to find growth, change and good in its wake. ▩

THE PARABLE OF THE
TANDOORI CHICKEN

My three children love Indian food. When they were young, my bringing home Indian food for dinner was one of their favorite treats. Being a creature of habit, on those occasions I would call our favorite Indian restaurant and have our order ready for me to pick up on my way home. My order always starts the same way: "One order of Tandoori chicken, very well done with sautéed onions and green peppers, and mild sauce." This has always worked beautifully. I would pick up the order. I would arrive home and ceremoniously announce I brought home Indian food. It was cooked to perfection. Daddy was a hero!

But one day it all went horribly wrong. This time, when I called the restaurant, I noticed the employee that answered the phone spoke very little English. It turns out she was a new member of the staff and unlike everyone else there who spoke fluent English, she was just learning. When I picked up the order I was fearful, but optimistic. I drove home, made my announcement, and we all sat down to eat. However, this time the order was completely wrong. It was in every way *not* what we wanted: the wrong dish, cooked the opposite of how we wanted it and with a sauce so hot I believe it spontaneously combusted in one's mouth. One by one, my children showed their disappointment. Well shy of hero status, I wasn't sure I would be allowed to sleep in the house that night.

So I started complaining about that employee: how she messed up, how she didn't speak enough English to do her job and how we would now have to find a new Indian restaurant because of her, and on and on. I complained and moaned and griped until finally my wife, who had been silent while I vented, simply said: "Why don't you just learn to say the order in her language?"

I stopped dead in my tracks. Why didn't I think of that? I was so busy being angry with the problem that I never thought about a solution. Here was an opportunity for me to remedy a problem instead of complain about it. In addition, it was an opportunity for *me* to learn something. All I needed to do was to *use* those words of Henry Ford: "Don't find fault. Find a remedy!" With a little effort, I could have solved a problem and ended up smarter to boot.

When we are confronted by students who "can't get it" or we can't get them to "want to get it," do we complain about the situation, or do we take those moments as opportunities to be a better teacher? Do we take kids where they are, the way they are, and figure out how to teach them?

You know, I still can't walk into that restaurant without grinning. That employee made me a better teacher and a better student. Every day, I wonder how many of those opportunities I miss.

Let us all remember the wonderful Zen proverb that goes something like this: "Inside or outside yourself you never have to change what you see, only the way you see it." We must always be on the lookout for our next chance to teach, our next chance to learn, our next chance to be the best teacher we can be.

FORTY-TWO STONES
AND AN EMPTY JAR

Ancient wisdom reminds us that today, this day, any day, is a gift. We can use it however we wish. But when it is over, it will be gone forever. We will have used it wisely or squandered it foolishly, but unquestionably we can never have it back again. All the more reason we should treasure every moment and savor its passing. Quite simply, we must cherish the promise of every new day.

To me, it's like an empty jar we get to fill as we see fit. Empty, it is full of promise. Ultimately, however, the value of the jar, like the day, is predicated on what we put in it. A sentiment as simple as it is brilliant, and all too often a lesson learned when the joys of youth have long passed. A lesson we can help teach our students in word and deed, remembering all the while the wonderful Spanish proverb that reminds us, "More things grow in the garden than the gardener sows." Many more things are learned in our classes than we set out to teach.

I like to think of every class just that way. Each one an empty jar—full of promise—which we get to fill as we see fit. Forty-two minutes for us to give as a gift to our students. Forty-two stones we get to put into our empty jar. As each minute passes, we are putting one stone in the jar. It is up to us to make each one valuable, worthwhile, rewarding and meaningful. It is up to us to decide what we put into that jar. It is up to us to fulfill the promise of each class, and in so doing help to fulfill the promise of each new day for our students.

I wish I were talented enough, or smart enough, that those stones could be made of gold. But I'm not. I can, however, make certain that though the stones I offer are simply garden-variety rocks, they are as clean, as smooth, and as polished as possible before I place them in that jar.

So the next time you start a class, picture an empty jar right next to you, and with the passing of every minute envision yourself placing one of those forty-two, or thirty, or ninety, or even three hundred sixty stones you are given into the jar, and choose prudently. Look into the eyes of those whom you teach and honor them, and our profession, with every one.

"When...?" or "When...!"

I t's all in a word. Or in this case, an inflection. Simply changing the way we say that one little word can make all the difference in the world. It can make our communication with a student positive and hopeful, or negative and defeatist. Every time we use that word we set up two possibilities: one optimistic, the other pessimistic.

Frustration and fatigue often lead us to use the latter if we're not careful, taking us down the path of being a negative influence in the classroom. However, the former provides us with a reinforcing and reassuring approach which fosters a positive environment. Can't you just hear statements like: "When are you going to stop talking?" Contrast that with: "When you are quiet in class it is so terrific!" How about: "When are you going to remember to indent every paragraph?" versus "When you indent the paragraphs your essay will look beautiful!"

The word *why*, though grammatically part of a question, can be used just as powerfully, reflecting a positive or negative attitude. Which of the following comments would you rather hear from your teacher? "Why aren't you following my directions?" or "Why don't I try saying it another way so it's easier for you to follow my directions?" "Why does that have to look so sloppy?" or "Why don't we try writing with our best penmanship?"

Every time we use either "when" or "why" we have the choice to be positive or negative. Every time we comment to our students we can couch it in a pessimistic or optimistic way. It seems so simple. In theory we all know it is. However, in the heat of the moment, with emotions flowing and frustration rearing its ugly head, which do we reach for? We must remember the one that will motivate our students better, and inspire them to improve. The answer is simple; remembering is hard; always following through is sometimes tremendously difficult. But *when* we do, we are all better teachers for having done so.

"Spoon-Feeding..."

Picture a scene: my mother and I having dinner at a wonderful five-star restaurant in New York City. We sit down to a lavish, gourmet meal served by waiters dressed in black tie and tails. After a lovely aperitif, our server brings us a breathtakingly beautiful tureen of crème d'haricots verts. Ah! Our imaginations run wild with excited anticipation.

Then, at the moment we begin to eat, my mom starts spoon-feeding me this lovely repast. There I sit, with her feeding me a spoonful at a time; spoonful after spoonful. At the very least, that would be an odd sight. Anyone watching would certainly be puzzled. Seemingly able to eat on my own, why would I need to be spoon-fed?

Now, change scenes completely. Picture me and my mother having dinner at our home when I was one year old. There we were with a baby-food jar of pureed string beans, Mom dutifully spoon-feeding me. That scenario sounds perfectly normal, doesn't it? The *only* difference between those two scenes is fifty-one years.

That is the essence of a marvelous quote by E. M. Forster: "Spoon-feeding in the long run teaches us nothing but the shape of the spoon," the words "long run" being what's vitally important. We all would agree that at the start of a very young person's educational career and many times during "new" learning adventures later in life, spoon-feeding is not only acceptable, it is necessary.

Whether due to a person's maturation level, inexperience, discomfort or uneasiness, we may need to spoon-feed much information. It is, however, our constant effort to wean students away from our spoon-feeding that makes all the difference. Just like my mom did for me with those pureed string beans, we spoon-feed our students so they get the nutrition they need, but then we encourage them to hold the spoon, play with the jar, mess around with the food, and in so doing, figure the whole thing out.

Can it be messy? Yes! Can pureed string beans end up on the kitchen walls? Yes! But what is the true purpose of education? Is it simply achieving a goal? No! That goal or knowledge must foster lifelong learning. We must teach them to *someday* be able to feed themselves with that spoon; then with a fork, a knife, chopsticks, and all other manner of feeding oneself. To borrow a sentiment from my dear friend, composer Reber Clark: The challenge of education is to make it point past itself. How incredibly true! It is only through our ever-vigilant dedication to "teaching" our students *how to learn*, and *how to teach themselves*, that our work will "point past itself."

Will that mean many moments of students trying to do something they find difficult? Would it often be easier to just spoon-feed that material? Sure. But in the words of John Stuart Mill, "The pupil who is never required to do what he cannot do, never does what he can do." *Then*, and quite possibly forever. So put on your apron, face mask and hip boots, and after you've spoon-fed your students enough to be healthy and happy, help them to learn how to feed themselves. Someday, when those very same students are "savoring" the knowledge and skills they possess, they will remember who taught them how to use that "spoon."

"If You've Told a Child..."

O n the great master list of what drives teachers crazy, certainly repetition would number in the top few. Repeating the same thing over and over again can be frustrating to say the least! Repeating the same thing over and over again can be frustrating to say the least! Repeating the same thing over and over again can be frustrating to say the least! (Sorry, I couldn't resist.)

I am not talking about the need for review or practice. I am referring to saying the same thing, time after time, trying to get a concept through to a student. For me, a simple test is whether I want to (though hopefully don't) start a comment with, "How many times do I have to tell you…!" That's the test. Something like, "Jimmy, (how many times do I have to tell you) the rule about 'i before e.'" Or, "Susan, (how many times do I have to tell you) the difference between infer and imply." Need I go on?

Yes, sometimes a little repetition is what Jimmy and Susan need to remind them of what they already know. But all too often they don't remember because they really don't understand. Maybe they just need to learn it a different way. In the words of Walter Barbe as quoted by William Purkey, "If you've told a child a thousand times, and the child still has not learned, then it is not the child who is the slow learner." Sometimes, those "Eureka!" moments when a student finally "gets it" are a result of its finally making sense after many repetitions, but we often can expedite that process by simply changing the way we teach.

It may not be a matter of the glass being half empty or half full, it may just be *the wrong size glass!* We might need to get a glass that fits the situation. When we can't catch a mouse with a trap, we can keep setting the trap with the same cheese every time it fails, or we can spend time trying to figure out what kind of cheese he may like better. It is often easier, or, maybe better put, a more natural instinct for us to do it *again* rather than try to figure out a way to do it *better*.

THE GOAL IS *NOT* TO BE UNDERSTOOD

W hat is the goal of a great communicator? The answer to that question has so many facets it would take volumes to do it justice. However, wouldn't you agree *getting the point across* — whatever that may be — is essential? If so, that goal could simply be stated as *being understood*. In other words, people *understood* what was being communicated; the communicator's intentions were *understood*. And what is a teacher, but a communicator? So being understood must be our goal. Right? Well, yes and no. Being understood is only part of the answer. Great communicators know they must go much further than that.

There is a wonderful old joke about a man parachuting from a burning airplane only to land in the middle of a massive, sprawling corn field in the heart of Iowa. As the man sits on the ground in a state of panic, trying to figure out what to do, he sees a person riding a bicycle along a road in the distance. Excitedly, the stranded man jumps up and yells to the bicycler, "Where am I?" To which comes the answer, "In the middle of a cornfield." The information in

the reply was perfectly correct, but equally and totally useless. The bicyclist gave a clear and meaningful answer that
was understood by the stranded man. The problem was the
man on the bike simply didn't know his audience.

As Stephen R. Covey wrote, we must "Seek first to understand, then to be understood." If our well-meaning bicycler
had simply taken the time to come to know the background
and situation of the person asking the question, he would
have been able to offer a response that was as useful as it was
understandable. As farfetched as this story is, it does point
to the source of a great deal of frustration for teacher and
student alike. The most well-intentioned, thought-out, and
expertly taught material is worthless to students who are not
ready or able to receive it. If they do not possess the mental, physical or emotional readiness to learn what is being
taught, it will not be understood, frustrating teachers who
are trying their best to teach, as much as the students who
are trying their best to learn. The problem is often not that
we taught it poorly, or we were *not* understood, but because
we simply didn't understand our audience. The better we understand our students, the better we can plan, sequence, prepare
and teach material that can — and thus will — be learned.
Whether it's a physical technique, an intellectual concept or
an emotional perception being taught, understanding who
our students are and where they came from is as important
as where we want them to go. Assessing the situation, and
understanding *them*, becomes far more important than being
understood. Great communicators know that, but also know
they must go further still.

Nearly two thousand years ago there lived a philosopher
by the name of Epictetus. Though he lived most of his

life in the first century A.D., it is amazing that his wisdom regarding this matter is as profound today as it was then. Wisdom — true wisdom — seems only to get better, or at least truer, with age. He cautioned, "Do not write so that you can be understood, write so that you cannot be misunderstood." A more perfect goal I can't imagine.

As teachers, how many of us have taught something *we* were sure our students understood? More important, something *our students* were sure they understood? Then upon evaluation we come to realize they didn't "get it" at all. Was it that they didn't understand? Sometimes, yes. But I believe it's far more likely that they *misunderstood*. Thinking of the advice of Epictetus, we probably taught the material so we were understood, *but not* so we couldn't be *misunderstood*. We knew what we wanted them to learn, but did they? Well, they thought they did. But sometimes, *what they understood* just wasn't *what we meant them to understand*.

It could have been the words we used as part of our instructions, which our students took to mean something different from that which we meant; physical gestures we made which they took as something very different from what we intended; or body language and facial expressions they read far differently from what we wished to imply. All these are simple misunderstandings. Scowls on our faces, complete with furrowed brows that result from our ardent concentration, can be misunderstood to mean disappointment. A teacher's loud voice can be misunderstood as communicating frustration, when it could be honest excitement and enthusiasm.

So perhaps our goal should be *first to understand*, and then to make certain we *can't be misunderstood*. Once we understand

our students, we must not just teach so we can be understood, but rather teach so we cannot be misunderstood.
Though that might sound like a game of semantics, it can
make all the difference in the world. A difference Epictetus
certainly understood. ▨

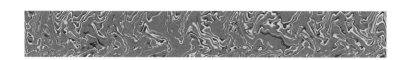

EXCELLENCE

W hat is excellence? How do you define that extraordinary ideal? When I think of excellence — true excellence — I think of the drive to do more than what is required, to do better than what is needed, and to go further than what is necessary. Not for the praise of others, but simply because our inner values, pride in our work, and willingness to go above and beyond dictate nothing less. And what always comes to mind is that magnificent "Lady" that adorns the New York City Harbor.

Seeing the Statue of Liberty from the ground or from the water is a grand and thrilling experience. One cannot help but to be struck with the beauty and power of the sculpture. The craftsmanship and detail of every facet of her crown, body, gown and face are truly remarkable. How can one look at her and not think the word "excellence"? However, flying down the Hudson River in an airplane or helicopter, soaring five hundred feet above that incredible monument, you see the *true* excellence of Lady Liberty.

From that vantage point, looking down on her head, you will see that every wisp, curl and strand of hair, as well as the back of her crown, was painstakingly fashioned to perfection. Every feature of that portion of the statue is as stunning — every detail as flawless — as the rest. Think of the hours of work that went into those remote areas. At first glance, it is easy to think of that as simply a reflection of the *talents* of the sculptor, Frederic Auguste Bartholdi. Well, it is far more than that! For you see, as far as he could have known, no one would ever see the top of the Statue of Liberty. No one.

Why? Because on October 28, 1886, when the great statue was dedicated by President Grover Cleveland, Orville and Wilbur Wright would still be seventeen years away from their historic flight of December 17, 1903. Though it's true the Mongolfier brothers had invented their hot air balloon some one hundred years before the Statue was made, realistically, Bartholdi probably thought only stray seagulls and pigeons would ever be the beneficiary of the exceptional efforts made to fashion the top of her head. In his mind, who would ever be able to look down on the statue from above to see the majesty of his work?

The sculptors, having no way of knowing that anyone would ever soar above their creation, still made the effort — gave of themselves — to make even those parts that would never be seen by any living soul, other than themselves, as beautiful and awe-inspiring as the rest. Why? Because their dedication to their craft allowed them to do nothing less. They sought not the adulation of others, but the *inner* knowledge that *they* gave their best effort, that their artistic pursuit was done as well as possible for no other reason than great art demanded it. Is that not the very definition of excellence? Is that not the essence of quality and taking pride in one's work?

Pushing ourselves and our students to understand, or, better put, having our students *come to understand* that simple thought, may be more important than anything we teach. What better gift can we give than sending all of our students off with that sense of integrity for their work? Searching for the smallest detail in the big picture may mean the difference between good and great. Work, even on seemingly insignificant minutia, may be the path to true excellence. As the great architect Ludwig Mies van der Rohe stated so eloquently, "God is in the details."

I also think of excellence in terms of what has become known as the "Butterfly Effect" theory of chaos, first put forth by Edward Lorenz. This concept is best known by the simple question he posed: "Does the flap of a butterfly's wings in Brazil set off a tornado in Texas?" The premise is that even the smallest detail or event, viewed individually as seemingly insignificant or random, can compound and in that way magnify and contribute to a much greater, even enormously powerful outcome.

An almost imperceptible happening can be the start of a pattern or string of events — one "feeding" off of or made possible by another — that can end up having great impact. I don't really know if the flap of a butterfly's wings in South America *can* cause a tornado in Texas, but I do know that even the smallest subtlety can sometimes be the spark that starts a chain of ever-intensifying focus and knowledge.

As one small impulse by a snake contributes to propel that animal through its serpentine movements, our attention to the details of our teaching and our students' learning helps propel our students to reach their potential.

The "what" of excellence — exemplified by those tiny details of The Lady of the Harbor which make her so perfect — coupled with the "why" of excellence — explained by "The Butterfly Effect" of how events can compound to become extremely compelling — reflect my belief that even the smallest detail of our work, and our students' attention to those details, matter greatly. They matter inestimably.

The more details we discover about our subject, the more we can attend to in our teaching. The more we attend to in our teaching, the more our students take with them through life. Ostensibly small details could be the nuance that makes for excellence. Not simply because of the attention to detail beyond the obvious, but because those events can be the catalyst for a chain of ever-increasingly vibrant learning.

Excellence, therefore, must be found in the obvious, but possibly more important, in the barely perceptible. There is no doubt that sometimes excellence in anything in life comes down to a simple phrase that reminds us that "Countless unseen details are often the only difference between mediocre and magnificent."

True excellence is attending to every detail, no matter how small or "unseen," because our commitment to education will allow nothing less. True excellence knows that those details can compound to create a "tornado" of impassioned learning. Education, in many ways, can be thought of as passing on to future generations the gift of knowing excellence, striving for excellence, appreciating excellence and living excellence. How magnificent! ▨

THE FLAMES OF
GROWTH

It is said that "Genius is the fire that lights itself." Well, I don't know about that, but I do believe that *learning* is *the fire that lights itself*. Finding excitement at the thought of *not* knowing, being curious as to how or why, having a willingness to take educational risks, believing in oneself and growing from mistakes is indeed a fire that lights itself. Simple curiosity starts a smoldering ash which grows into a fire that is *knowing more*.

Isn't that true learning? Isn't that what each of us wants our students to come to know? Of course we want to help them learn facts; education requires a certain amount of that. But, of greater worth, don't we want to give them a foundation — a burning desire — for learning? Don't we want them to learn to *want to learn*, learn *to learn*, and come to realize that the *pursuit* of knowledge and ability starts with not just admitting, but relishing the thought of not having an answer?

"I Don't Know."

I was recently teaching a graduate seminar course at the university. During one specific class, after I had just finished giving each student a topic to research for the next class, one of the students posed a question related to something we had discussed earlier that night. I was stymied — truly baffled. After thinking for a minute, I admitted my ignorance and told the class I now had *my* homework. And I guess as I said it my enthusiasm for learning must have shown. As my students saw their teacher thrilled at the joy of not knowing, one of them said, "Look at you all excited!" I was. I was truly beaming. Three little words set me on my way. Just like the saying goes, "All learning begins with the simple phrase, 'I don't know.'" Or as Socrates stated so clearly, "Wisdom begins in wonder."

That reminds me of a story. Years ago, a friend of mine stood for his doctoral oral exams. He sat in a room filled with professors from many disciplines. One after another, these learned scholars fired questions designed to challenge my friend's knowledge. All, that is, but one teacher, who just sat there listening. He said nothing and asked nothing. Finally, after all the teachers were satisfied, the committee chair asked if anyone had anything further. My friend saw light at the end of the tunnel when out of the blue that silent professor announced he had one question. He looked my friend in the eyes and said, "Tell me about John Irving Gemini III, listing his greatest accomplishments in order of importance."

My friend said his heart fell to the pit of his stomach as fear and trepidation flowed through his being. Not only did my friend not know the man's accomplishments in order of importance, he had never even heard of him. At that moment, my friend thought about trying to — how should I say — make something up, but thought better of it. Instead, he reflected a minute and proceeded to admit, sadly, that he did not know of the gentleman or his contributions. "But," he went on to say, "by the time the sun sets tonight, I will know everything there is to know about him and here's how," whereupon he stated, chapter and verse, how he would research the information.

The professor listened patiently, then responded by saying, "A rather good answer given the fact I made him up five minutes ago." After the inquisition (I mean oral exam) was over, my friend cornered the professor, asking why he did what he did. The response was as awesome as the question was calculated: "With as much as you know," he said, "I just wanted to make certain you learned the most important lesson: saying 'I don't know.'" In the words of Chuang Tzu, "He who knows he is confused is not in the worst confusion."

"The ancestor of every action is a thought," Ralph Waldo Emerson tells us. It is simply a matter of whether we seize, and act upon, those thoughts that are fertile questions, and do so with delight. Roger Lewin said, "Too often we give children answers to remember rather than problems to solve." Certainly, we must do some of both, but don't you agree the answers we get through our own *endeavors of curiosity* become some of the most precious answers we learn? Getting students to perceive questions, to rejoice in the fact they *don't* have the answers, and to be equipped with the necessary tools for discovery, must number among the greatest gifts a teacher can give. Relishing in having the answer is one thing; relishing in *not* having the answer may be even better.

Believing in Themselves

James Russell Lowell asserted that "More men fail through ignorance of strength than through knowledge of their weakness." That is probably true, but I would contend even more people fail from a *lack of confidence* in their ability than through ignorance of strengths. In the words of Ralph Hodgson, "Some things have to be believed to be seen."

To that end, we must help instill that confidence *in our students*, getting them to truly believe in themselves. Telling them *we* have confidence in them is a first step. But "putting our money where our mouth is" by acting on that confidence is of even greater value. Giving students educational responsibilities, decisions to make, and tasks to perform goes a long way toward voting our confidence.

If that confidence is not instilled, the "knowledge of weakness" from the quote above quickly and firmly can become a conviction. Students then start to believe in their weaknesses more than their abilities to overcome them. They will, quite sadly, live the words of Richard Bach: "Argue for your limitations, and you get to keep them."

Take Risks Rather Than Play it Safe.

"The greatest mistake you can make in life," warns Elbert Hubbard, "is to be continually fearing you will make one." Have truer words ever been spoken? How sad is it to see people, especially young people, so worried about making a mistake that they never put themselves in a position to make one. And by so doing, rarely taste failure, but virtually doom themselves to horizons that are in close reach.

To be so afraid of mistakes that one becomes educationally frozen—paralyzed by fear—is debilitating to say the least. As David Grayson states, "We fail more often by timidity than by over-daring."

How noble is the goal of helping every student understand Frederick B. Wilcox's advice: "Progress always involves risks. You can't steal second base and keep your foot on first." Or André Gide's version of the same sentiment: "One does not discover new lands without consenting to lose sight of the shore for a very long time." It comes down to realizing, as James Thurber says, "You might as well fall flat on your face as lean over too far backward." But the thought which most vividly describes the realization I hope each of my students comes to know is from Søren Kierkegaard: "To dare is to lose one's footing momentarily. Not to dare is to lose oneself."

Is it scary to put yourself out on a limb? Yes, but as Frank Scully questions, "Why not go out on a limb? Isn't that where the fruit is?" But James Bryant Conant may have summed it up most elementally: "Behold the turtle. He makes progress only when he sticks his neck out." I want only to ask every student and every teacher one question, posed by Robert H. Schuller: "What great thing would you attempt if you knew you could not fail?" How liberating it is to know the value of educational risk, be willing to take those risks, and derive pleasure from taking them.

Learn from Mistakes

"Failure is success if we learn from it," says Malcolm S. Forbes. Indeed. The joy of making mistakes is in learning from them, growing as a result of information gained from those mistakes. We must help students to grow and develop *from* mistakes, not *in spite* of them. With our guidance they will value what they learn from attempts that don't work as much as from those that do. It's simple: "Take risks: if you win, you will be happy; if you lose, you will be wise." To me, what fans that "fire" of education was best proclaimed by the remarkable Pablo Picasso when he humbly affirmed, "I am always doing that which I cannot do, in order that I may learn how to do it."

Then Risk Again

Armed with information gleaned from our mistakes, we must be willing — no, excited — to risk again, and again and again, learning more with every attempt. In that way the cycle of growth continues ever further. But to what end? What is the goal? Well, I think H. Jackson Brown, Jr. said it best: "A successful life doesn't require that we've done the best, but that we've done our best."

How powerful three little words can be. Three little words that can change a life. Three little words that can change the world—or at least our tiny part of it. Three little words that hold the key to learning. So every time you have helped a student to say or to think those words—"I don't know"—realize you were the flint for their steel, that made a spark, that lit a fire of learning. The fire of learning that lights itself. ▨

"Far Better it is to Dare Mighty Things..."

"Far better it is to dare mighty things, to win glorious triumphs even though checkered by failure, than to rank with those timid spirits who neither enjoy nor suffer much because they live in the gray twilight that knows neither victory nor defeat." Every time I think of those words of former President Theodore Roosevelt, I am almost paralyzed by their tremendous power. To me they are the perfect description of a teacher. Isn't the essence of what we do every day to "dare mighty things" for each of our students?

It doesn't matter whether we are teaching advanced concepts to high school students, or teaching the first steps of learning a skill to first graders. We teach our students to dare mighty things. However, it is the teaching of that very life lesson which is most important. By our teaching we help them to learn to dare mighty things of themselves now, and to continue to do so for all the days of their lives, in every aspect of life. Basically, we teach them to dream big dreams.

But how can we teach them to dream big? Well I believe it happens in three steps. First we dream for them. Then we inspire them to start dreaming for themselves, helping them discover that *what is possible* only comes from *dreaming*. Finally we get them not just to dream, but to dare mighty dreams: to take risks for dreams that are worthwhile, knowing failure may be the short-term price we pay.

Dream for Them

To borrow a sentiment from Mark Twain: A regular person is someone who does things because they *have* been done before. A teacher is someone who does things because they *haven't* been done before. We see students as what they are, but know that each of them must become what he or she can become.

Many of our students will come to us looking for goals, seeking a dream, but having no idea of what or how. In that case, we can dream for them. We as teachers thrive on that challenge as every day we live those words of George Bernard Shaw, made famous by former President John F. Kennedy: "You see things; and you say 'Why?' But I dream things that never were; and I say 'Why not?'" But we also know that dreaming for those students is only a start.

It is acting on those dreams with our hard work and dedication that can make them a reality. As Joel Barker held, "Vision without action is merely a dream. Action without vision just passes the time. Vision with action can change the world." That's right, "change the world," or at least our little piece of it. And because of the limitless impact we have on our students now, and, through them, generations we will never know, we can truly change a bigger part of the world than we may ever realize. The boundaries of a teacher's inspiration and influence know no limits of time or place.

Inspire Them to Start to Dream for Themselves

Though a necessary start, our dreaming for our students is nothing more than a catalyst: the spark to light a fire. The fuel that will burn for their lifetimes, however, must come from them if it is to be true and long-lasting. But how do we start to encourage those first steps of dreaming? I believe we do it just as we would any other aspect of our teaching, whether it is for knowledge or for an attitude: we take every opportunity to exude excitement and promise.

No better words exist to portray this than those of William Purkey when he wrote that the remarkable Leo Buscaglia "used the metaphor of knowledge being a marvelous feast. What the teacher can do is prepare food with great relish and care, sample it frequently, dance around the table at mealtime, and invite students to join the celebration!"

If we want our students to fulfill those words of Robert Louis Stevenson, "To be what we are, and to become what we are capable of becoming, is the only end of life," then we must get them to understand, as Carl Sandburg said, "Nothing happens unless first a dream." What a valuable lesson that is for every child to learn. They must learn to cultivate dreams of whom and what they wish to become. As Ariel Francos put so succinctly, "It's not what you are. It's what you want to be."

Is that a frightening thought for any young person? Is moving down that path a difficult choice? Is deciding to take those first steps of dreaming like walking through an open door into a dark, unknown room? Yes. But our students need to learn that "we cannot become what we need to be by remaining what we are." Sometimes that fear can be debilitating, causing many to feel it is safer to stay as they are than to risk dreaming of being more. I answer that with the words of Seneca: "It is not because things are difficult that we do not dare, it is because we do not dare that they are difficult."

Get Them to Dare Mighty Dreams

Once our students have started to think in terms of possibilities rather than probabilities, and taken those first steps of dreaming for themselves, we must urge them to start dreaming bigger dreams. After experiencing the freedom and exhilaration of dreaming, and the success that comes from steps (no matter how small) along the path to our dreams, they need to be coaxed into envisioning even mightier dreams. They must dare to think in terms they once thought unattainable, realizing that "only those who attempt the absurd achieve the impossible." Or as T. S. Eliot put it, "Only those who will risk going too far can possibly find out how far one can go."

Sometimes it's not envisioning *how far* we need to travel that becomes our mission but envisioning another path to get us there. That straight line we *think* is the best way to our mighty dream may be tried and true, but may not be the safest, best or most beautiful route. Often it is more about dreaming up a better mousetrap than how to get more mousetraps. Wonderful will be the moment when our students grow to understand and live by those poignant words of Ralph

Waldo Emerson, "Do not follow where the path may lead; go instead where there is no path and leave a trail."

Whether it's learning to dare to go further or to dare to go a different way, the bottom line is for them to dream what they never imagined achievable so they can achieve what they only dreamed imaginable. As C. S. Lewis stated so exquisitely, "Aim at Heaven and you will get Earth thrown in. Aim at Earth and you get neither."

Once we get our students to dream big dreams, the largest challenge we face is to keep them focused on those dreams despite any setback, lack of momentum or temporary failure. They need to keep their eyes on the prize: the goal at the end of that dream. We must convince them that the small bumps along the road don't guide our path, they make it interesting. Like a racehorse wearing blinders so as not to get distracted by passing horses, our students need to ignore the distractions of disappointment, staying focused on the goal at the finish line.

If they turn back, quit or change course simply because the path gets difficult, or because others decide to go different ways, they will never discover their true potential. I think Omar Bradley said it best: "We need to learn to set our course by the stars, not by the lights of every passing ship." Those passing ships in life do offer light, but the beacon of the stars must always be the guide to that place where dreams help shape the destiny of our students.

Final Thoughts

Why do we need to dream for our students and teach them to dream? Simply because if we don't, quite possibly no one ever will. Inspiring our students to dream gives them the liberty to become ever more perfectly what essentially they are. We can help them to *truly* understand the words of former President Woodrow Wilson when he said, "We grow great by dreams. All big men are dreamers. They see things in the soft haze of a spring day or in the red fire of a long winter's evening. Some of us let these great dreams die, but others nourish and protect them; nurse them through bad days till they bring them to the sunshine and light which comes always to those who sincerely hope that their dreams will come true." In that way they will learn to dare to dream, and nourish and protect *their* dreams until they see the sunshine of their tomorrows.

As with a diamond, each single facet of their dreaming and "daring" may be modest in value, but the combination of the facets becomes priceless — just like them! As Sir Winston Churchill stated so superbly, "We make a living by what we get, we make a life by what we give." What better to give our students than the gift of dreams? What better indeed!

I would like to close with a poem that was given to me some years ago by a student in one of my classes. In its simplicity we can find the hopes of all those whom we teach.

Shoot for the Moon

That time you asked me to shoot for the moon,
I knew it was important to you,
So I did,
But I failed.

That time you asked me to shoot for the moon,
You told me to try,
So I did,
And I failed.

That time you asked me to shoot for the moon,
I tried again because you made it sound so good,
And I did,
But I failed.

That time you asked me to shoot for the moon,
You lifted me half way there,
So I did,
And I failed.

That time you asked me to shoot for the moon,
Was only the first of many,
That I did,
But to fail.

That time you asked me to shoot for the moon,
Ended up being the start of a journey,
Though I failed,
But I did.

That time you asked me to shoot for the moon,
Showed me the way,
But to dream,
So I did.

And now that I've been there many times,
Though some I did fail,
That time you asked me to shoot for the moon,
Was the day I truly learned how.

ROUTINE CAN BE COMFORTABLE — AND DEADLY

I was sitting on an airplane, waiting to be de-iced; the airplane, that is. The flight attendant promptly turned on the automated preflight safety briefing. You know, the one describing rules and procedures in the event of an emergency. Flying as much as I do, I stopped listening to that *routine* lecture decades ago. What they do and say is set. It is pat. It is the exact same thing on every flight. No, I'm not minimizing its importance. In fact, if I am ever on a flight that has a catastrophe, I'm sure somewhere in my last thoughts will be, "What did they tell me to do?" Followed promptly by, "Why didn't I listen to those briefings more carefully!"

On this flight, however, partway through the first sentence of the briefing, the recording started to skip and repeat like an old vinyl record album stuck on the same word over and over. The flight attendant reset the announcement and tried again. It jammed at the same spot.

She then tried three more times. Still not working, she resorted to the outdated, now obsolete, speech over the intercom using a microphone. On this small airplane, there was only one flight attendant and the only microphone was a telephone-like handset. Knowing what she had to do, she opened her manual to the required speech, took a deep breath and prepared to do it the old-fashioned way. She had to read the announcement while holding the handset between her head and shoulder, because she had to keep her hands free to demonstrate the seatbelt, flotation device and oxygen mask. Needless to say, it was pretty rough. With all the telephone holding and demonstrating, she stumbled over and over again with the reading. She was fighting a losing battle to continually find her place in the manual after each demonstration, all the while trying to hold the phone in place.

After a few moments of dropping the phone and getting lost, she decided to just plain "wing it" (no pun intended). She used normal everyday language, and joked with us, rather than reciting the pat text given so routinely by the automated system. It was wonderful! I listened to every word. Was there anything really different about the information we were given? No. Was the material better or more correct? Surely not. But because it was not the routine, I glued my attention to her every word.

By now, you are probably wondering what this could possibly have to do with teaching. Let me try to explain. We all need routine in our lives. It provides us with structure and security. It allows us to do reoccurring things faster, easier and more efficiently. The redundancy of doing whatever it is over and over again, the same way each time, allows us to get very good and very fast at accomplishing that task. Most important, it allows us to do it without much thought. We can do it on autopilot. Change that routine and the results can be frustrating and debilitating. For example, if you asked me to put my belt on my pants, threading it to the right, I could do it. Sadly, it would take me about three days, and the belt would be wrapped around my neck and right thigh, but I could do it! Why? Because for more than five decades I have threaded my belt to the left, and that routine has allowed me to put my belt on each day without even giving it a thought.

In our classes, as positive and productive as some routines can be in providing effective procedures and efficient outcomes, those very routines can be mind numbing, fostering actions done as if on autopilot. If routine allows students to know a series of activities or drills so well they can do them thoughtlessly, they probably are not even attending to what they are doing. Though surely repetition and review are essential in education, it is the fine line between routine and variety that may make the difference as to whether students are careful or careless, casual or concerned, indifferent or determined. It is not necessarily the *what* of our teaching, but the *how* that makes routine a problem, for mindlessness negates attentiveness and focus.

If we simply vary our routines and use a variety of approaches, techniques and materials, we will keep our classes fresh and encourage students not to work "on autopilot." They will concentrate their attention on us the way I did on my distressed flight attendant, rather than tune out the way I do with those prerecorded announcements. Is it correct for me to ignore those recordings? No. Is it correct for students to mindlessly do an exercise or activity? Possibly. But human nature being what it is, we must provide an environment that encourages concentration and rigorous attention at every turn. As F. M. Alexander taught, "Change involves carrying out an activity against the habit of life."

Does anyone intend for the students they teach to go through their paces in a routine manner? Of course not. Can some element of routine be valuable and productive in the classroom, facilitating structure and providing comfort? Absolutely. However, if not watched carefully, that routine can become deadly to the attention and focus of student and teacher alike. Somewhere, that flight attendant is traveling the skies. She probably hopes to forget that flight, not knowing I'll always remember it. ▨

ONE MOMENT
OF ANGER

So there I was, in the middle of a rehearsal with my University Band. It could just as easily have been a math class, science lab or third-grade reading lesson. We were working on a technically difficult passage of very short, extremely fast, pointillistic sounds that were being passed around the ensemble like gunfire. The problem was it sounded as if the students were all at the firing range wearing blindfolds! It was amazing to me that after ninety minutes of hard work, this passage was getting the better of us. I did what any teacher would do: I rehearsed that short section with determination. It got worse. So I tried doing it with a very intense, dogmatic drive that surely should have focused their concentration. It got worse.

I reached into my bag of tricks and decided to back off and lightheartedly rehearse the passage with a casual "come on guys let's see what we can do" attitude. Need I tell you how that went? Again, I reached into my bag of tricks, this time so far that I hit floor. After what seemed like a decade of trying different techniques which included everything but my attempting to juggle, I started to feel as though the only thing left, the last resort, was for me to get cantankerous. I began rehearsing with that nasty tone of voice, and after a few moments of it succeeding like the voyage of the *Titanic*, I stopped dead in my tracks, and decided on a different path: they needed a story.

I stopped the group firmly and with no explanation began my saga. "Years ago," I said with a knowing grin, "I was away conducting in a very small, absolutely beautiful town in the middle of nowhere. I mean nowhere. I mean the 'big city' closest to nowhere was still in the middle of nowhere!" After a wonderful performance, I continued, one of the other conductors and I needed to stay over an extra night before we could fly home. After talking with several folks from the community, we decided to take in a movie at the local cinema. In the center of this wonderful town, this beautiful old movie theater from a long-gone era still had a pit for the orchestra.

Worried this little theater wouldn't have refreshments, we decided to grab some candy from a general store next door. Though we had only met a few days before, the other conductor and I made short order of choosing our treat: *Peanut M&M's.* Not a small bag, or a large bag, or even the extra-large bag. We bought the jumbo bag; you know, the "no-two-human-beings-should-ever-be-able-to-eat-this-much-candy-in-one-sitting" size bag! Proud of our efforts, we went to the theater and sat down in the very back of the hall. Having no willpower, we decided it was time to break into the candy. I was assigned the easy task of opening the bag. Holding each side of the top of the bag, I pulled in opposing directions. My gentle tug didn't succeed. I pulled a bit more firmly. That too failed. So I tugged with even more force, it turns out with *just enough* force to rip the bag completely open, and I do mean completely. At that moment, every single M&M fell to the very steeply sloped cement floor and began to roll toward the front of the theater. After the initial shock of those sweet gems hitting the floor, and the blood-curdling stare from my "partner-in-candy," I thought I was in the clear as I sat there mortified with embarrassment. I was wrong. The "fun" was still to come.

To my horror, every single piece of the "no-two-human-beings-should-ever-be-able-to-eat-this-much-candy-in-one-sitting" size bag rolled to the front of the hall in a massive race for freedom, then began the downward fall six feet onto the cement floor of the orchestra pit below. No words can describe what that waterfall of M&M's sounded like. Trust me, it was awful. It was like a million little points of sound attacking at random. "Now," I continued, "what could my little story have to do with this rehearsal, you ask? The way you are playing that passage sounds just like my M&M's." After a few moments of laughter, we tried the passage again.

It was perfect. I even repeated it to make sure it wasn't luck; again it was perfect. Why? How? I gave no instructions, I gave no corrective information, I did nothing but make them laugh and get them to envision how bad their original execution of those measures sounded. It wasn't just that the pressure was off; I had tried that to no avail. It wasn't because of the brief respite from rehearsing it; I had tried that too. All I know is within seconds of hearing that dumb story it was beautiful.

That rehearsal reminded me that we should move toward our goal sometimes by running at full speed, sometimes by walking, sometimes by heading straight to it, and sometimes by going a roundabout way. But sometimes, no matter whether it's a rehearsal, or that math class, science lab or reading lesson, the trick may be that however we get there, we should get there laughing. It beats surly most every time. As the Chinese proverb goes, "It is better to laugh at one moment of anger than to regret all the moments to come."

When that evening's rehearsal was over, I stood in the band room talking with several graduate students as the hall emptied. As we were chatting, the rehearsal room doors opened and in ran two sophomores from the band: two of my pride and joy. They proceeded to run over and give me two jumbo bags of *Peanut M&M's*, saying, "Here, we ran out and got these to make up for the ones you lost!" I was overwhelmed. It's amazing, just when I am sure I truly appreciate my students and know how incredible they are, they outdo themselves. I didn't know whether to laugh or cry. So after they left, on my way home, I did both.

After eating an entire bag, I kept the wrapper. I use it to this day in the session I present on motivation, discipline and inspiration. It will always remind me of them, of how lucky I am to have had such wonderful students to share my life with, and of the day I chose a better path.

THE 33 P'S OF A WONDERFUL CLASS

This chapter is based on a workshop I have had the pleasure of presenting over many years. It is one of my favor-
ites because the person who gets the most out of it every time,
is me. It reminds me of the teacher I want to be. The person
and the personality that I truly want my students to come to
know. It always reminds me of goals I have lost touch with,
ideas I have forgotten to use, or convictions I have let slip
away. It does, however, have the worst title imaginable.

Before first presenting this session, I recall sitting with
a group of my graduate students. I was asked what the title
was. After describing it, one young lady chimed in and
said that she was going to develop one called "The 33 D's."
I thought for a moment, then responded that I couldn't
come up with thirty-three words that started with the letter D that had to do with teaching. Paraphrasing her, she
then started in with the likes of: Those *darn* word problems,
those *darn* formulas, those *darn* punctuation marks! Though
I have tried to come up with a better title, I have failed to
find one that captures the purpose.

What follows is simply a collection of thoughts. There is nothing new here. You already know and do them. These are the qualities that make you a dedicated, vibrant and sincere educator. They are presented to remind you of the many great things you do every day in your own way. My only suggestion is to check that it is truly happening the way you think it is by regularly videotaping your classes.

So often I will watch a videotape of one of my classes and see that what I thought I had done was not what I truly did. What I wanted to do *and was sure I had done* was not apparent on the tape. I was certain I did a specific thing, but didn't see it once in that hour-long class. By videotaping ourselves we can objectively say, "Yes, I can count seven times in the first twenty minutes of that class that I reinforced positive behaviors." That way we know we *are* doing it. Not that we *want* to do it, or *think* we are doing it, but that we actually are doing it. That becomes the true barometer of what we do and how we do it. If you don't videotape yourself, you may be missing out on one of the great joys of teaching. To watch a tape and think, "Why did I say that?" allows me a chance to fix the problem before I repeat it. I can realize that I was so worried about the penmanship of the first row of students that I missed the fact that two young people in the back row were dueling with rulers. Whatever it is, we can assess so much, and make corrections during the very next class. Our growth and the progress of our students will increase immensely.

When lawyers are trained, they must study countless hours of actual trials. They study every word and maneuver with the hopes of copying what works and not replicating what fails. That is what we need to do on a regular basis.

The benefits of that sometimes-intimidating process are remarkable.

Purpose

Simply, that we have goals which are clearly defined. Not just that we are going to "work with" the kids five days a week for one hundred eighty days. We must define those goals for the students from the very beginning. What concepts should they learn? "By the end of this year I want them to do the following." We may disagree on what the *that* is. But it doesn't matter to me as much *what* it is, but that we can *document* what it is. Then, as we go along, we can assess whether students are meeting those goals. At the end of a day, week, marking period or year we are able to see where they are in relation to our goals. You can firmly say, "They met my goals." Or, "I fell a bit short here, this is what we need to work on more." The key is that there are clearly defined goals rather than just "winging it" day after day.

I often receive phone calls from teachers asking my opinion of a specific aspect of course content. I always frustrate them by responding that they are asking an unanswerable question. Without knowledge of their goals, there is no way to answer the question of whether that, or any, content is appropriate. I liken this to someone walking up to you and asking, "Give me your opinion, I'm thinking of getting an appendectomy." To answer that question you need to know if their appendix is inflamed. If they're having a problem with their liver, an appendectomy isn't going to do a darn thing. So unless we know what the goals are, we can't match the material or techniques to them.

Plan

Once we have defined our goals, we should detail the sequence in which concepts should be taught. We can prioritize them so it makes sense for us. Do I want them to understand "x" before they learn "y"? And if I do, which permutations of the use of "x" do I want them to understand? Think about that; for there is probably a real justification for that answer, one way or the other. We have to decide, because the material has to match our goals as we prioritize them. We have to set schedules for the day, for the month, for the year, and indeed, for the entire school program of study for that discipline.

This is quite simply making certain you have a detailed, district-wide, subject-specific curriculum. It is the only way to gain consensus on goals, materials and methodology across grades and areas of study. It is the only way to weather change. Those changes of faculty, as well as changes of students from grade to grade, and area to area of specialization within the discipline. This may take many hours of meetings (over vast quantities of coffee) but we need to hash this out and come to agreement as to what will be taught and when. You may feel that certain tasks should be learned by eighth grade, while some of your colleagues may feel that other tasks would be better. Once it is debated and agreed to, each teacher will know where the students are to be at every stage of their training. This understanding should include concepts, materials, methodologies and every other aspect of the program. If it is clearly understood that by the eighth grade all students will have a basic grasp of certain information, then all involved know what the expectation is and can meet it accordingly.

To that end, we must ask if we always use a lesson plan. Many say to me that they've taught for so many years that they don't need a lesson plan. They know where they are going. I think there is some truth to that. Though I always respond by saying that I've done this a fair number of years and I still won't walk into a class without one. Granted, a lot of them are made up of one-word blurbs that only mean something to me. Heaven forbid I died before the class, in that no one would know what was to be taught. That one word, however, is enough to spark my memory as to what I want to accomplish.

Even the finest teachers I have ever observed had a lesson plan. Though it more resembled a list, it was still a lesson plan. It was like a punch-list, no different than you would give a builder doing a project in your home. Do this, then this, then this. At those moments I can't help but think, "If it's good enough for them, I think I should do this forever." Again, it could just be a little outline. But I think we have to have something, for if we don't, we are just ad-libbing, and ad-libbing always scares me because it usually wastes time. Time is one thing we don't *have* to waste. Think about it this way: if we have thirty-three students in front of us in a class and we waste even one minute, the compound effect can be staggering. Multiply that one minute of wasted time by the thirty-three members of the class, and you have the number of man-hours lost. If we have five of those wasted minutes in a class, we have to multiply that number of man-hours lost by five to get the amount of time wasted in just one class. Multiply that by a week, let alone a year, and think of the time lost. Whenever I think of that formula, I am over-whelmed by the magnitude of its power. It makes me ever conscious of every second of time during every class period.

Pedagogy

The phrase I always think of when it comes to pedagogy is: "Why is it that there is never enough time to do things right…but always enough time to do them over?" How often I have forgotten the pedagogy behind what we do in the haste of doing it. How often I have "taught" some-thing to a class, only to find out I got through the material, but didn't really teach it, because they didn't really learn it. They learned it well enough to pass a test, but did they truly come to understand it? Could they apply what they learned? Could they transfer it to new situations? We need remember that simply being able to do something or being exposed to something doesn't necessarily mean that it is learned.

I often think of the notion of a bandage versus a cure when it comes to teaching. When there is a lack of under-standing do we solve it with a quick fix, like a bandage, or do we seek to understand what is needed to cure the patient? In education, bandages can be useful when we need them, but only if we remember to go back and teach the concept so that gap in the students' learning doesn't stay with them.

Possible

By this I mean, is it possible? We need to make certain that what we are asking students to do is possible, realistic, achievable and appropriate. Do they possess the readiness as well as the mental, physical and emotional maturity to accomplish what we want them to achieve? Lofty goals are wonderful, but only if they are grounded in the realities of readiness and maturity. How often are students asked to perform tasks or learn information that is so far out of reach that failure is the only possible outcome? I am not saying we shouldn't challenge our students, or give them tasks that at times are a stretch, for certainly that is one way to encourage them to grow. I am saying that a challenge can be a positive experience, but being swamped yields frustration and discouragement.

Practice

It has long been said that "practice makes perfect." However, far more correct is that "perfect practice makes perfect." Though it is true we need to get students to practice what they have learned for it to become a part of them, sadly, all too often that takes the shape of students simply going through their paces. When that happens, their homework of "practicing" what they have learned becomes inattentive, mindless "getting through it" which at best fosters sloppiness and at worst has them practicing the wrong thing.

Whether it is practicing a technique well but using it at the wrong time, practicing a task with shortcuts that will prevent transfer of the skill to later uses, practicing a series of actions in the wrong order, or practicing higher level skills without attention to basic operations, we all know the quality of practice matters far more than the quantity of practice. We can foster that notion with more targeted practice objectives and greater attention to *how* students practice, remembering that the quantity of practice only matters if the quality of that practice is finely honed. Basically it comes down to getting our students to practice the right things at the right times in the right ways for the right reasons.

Position

Simply put, can they see you? Are there obstacles to visual communication between teacher and students caused by our position in the room, our students' positions in the room, or the room itself? Lack of lighting, where kids have to strain to see the teacher is one such obstacle. As well, often we set up our classrooms so that students are staring directly into sunlight coming through a bank of windows. Their squinting tells us they are looking right into the surface of the sun. Unless we take the opportunity to occasionally walk over to see their perspective, we might miss that problem. Poles, columns, railings, cabinets and the like offer physical obstacles to sight which we grow accustomed to having in the way. Simple adjustments can make a world of difference. My favorite story about sight obstacles comes from an experience I had while in Europe.

I was rehearsing a high school concert band in a new, all wood, cathedral ceiling band room. The wall against which the conductor stood was all glass. That room was extraordinary. It was nicer than any mountain retreat one could ask for. So I started to rehearse. As I conducted, I watched these students look around in bewildered awe. I stopped to ask for their attention. As I continued, if anything, the problem got worse. I couldn't figure out the dilemma until I turned around and looked out those giant windows. There in front of me was a magnificent, astounding, startling, overwhelming view of the Alps. The Alps! There stood before us those monuments of nature towering in the sunlight. They were breathtaking. Not wanting to compete with that view, I immediately stopped them, and said, "Gang, guess what we're going to do? We're going to get up and reset the ensemble facing the opposite direction." At that moment, without missing a beat, one young man blurted out: "What, so you get to look at the Alps!"

These and a multitude of other obstacles to communication in our classrooms are detriments to learning to which we become oblivious over time.

Preparation

We must truly know our material. Kids know when we're "faking it" and they know when we have the material down cold. They also know when we make a mistake because we aren't well prepared versus when we simply make a mistake. Lord knows I've made more than my fair share of mistakes during my classes, but students seem to be forgiving of them as long as they know I am prepared. But, they are never willing to forgive faking it, nor should they. Though we know we can learn the material as the students do, staying two feet ahead of them, we also know that means their progress resembles a leapfrog game with our staying just out in front.

Think how much more progress can result from your *starting* miles ahead of them in preparation, pulling them to you, always staying leagues ahead. When people question the necessity of this for young students, I ask them to try it once. Learn even one lesson cold. Then go into your class. It's addictive. You become addicted to being that well prepared, that much in control, and that productive. You will see this enormous growth in those fifth or sixth graders, realize what you got them to do, and come to the conclusion it is nothing short of amazing. You will realize you knew every problem they had before they had them. You'll know that you got things fixed by getting in their faces before they knew they were having problems. You then come to think if that could happen every day, their rate of progress would be awesome. I liken it to studying for a test. If you go into an exam having not really studied, you hesitantly work to gnaw off every question with fear and trepidation. If you have truly studied, you boldly take the exam and find it refreshing, exciting and strangely enjoyable.

My favorite quote about truly knowing our material comes from Sun-Tzu in the book *The Art of War*. (I'm not trying to compare classes to war, though sometimes it may feel that way!) He states, "Every battle is won before the war." It is so true. If you go into a class knowing the lesson and information cold, I guarantee you that you will win. It is going to be a great class. It's got to be; the deck is rigged in your favor. If we go in "improvising," I will likewise guarantee that we will eventually lose. You, the kids, the class, the whole experience won't be as good. Louis Pasteur summed this up better than anybody. He had no idea because he was too busy discovering scientific wonders, but he was right on the mark for excellence in teaching through true preparation when he said, "...chance favors the prepared mind." If you know the material well, you can then find something hiding within it and say, "Look at this fantastic thing I realized." Conversely, if you are so busy in class figuring out what to do next, you're not in any way going to be ready to recognize the little bits of neat stuff, often the genius, buried in the information or technique, waiting to be stumbled upon or discovered. If your mind is prepared, chance will favor it!

Abraham Lincoln once said, "If I was given an axe and was told that I had eight hours to cut down a tree, I would spend six hours sharpening the axe." A teacher who is winging it is spending sixteen hours with a dull axe pounding away for naught, when he or she could spend forty-two minutes with a keenly sharpened axe and get a whole heck of a lot done. Just think about that before you go to your next class.

Pearl

I believe that in every class we need to make one beautiful pearl. I use a pearl as my model because it is perfect. It has a perfect beginning, perfect middle and perfect end. It's just this one little thing and it's perfect. In and of itself it isn't much, but it *is* perfect. I believe that when we teach, we need to give our students this beacon. It may be one equation, one rhyme, one activity. It can be something tiny. But it has to be as perfect as we are capable of achieving. If we can get them to successfully do that one thing, then we can stop them, ask them to realize what they just did, speak of how spectacular it was, and get completely jazzed about it.

That pearl does two things: first, it gives them an example of your expectations. How many of us have been in classrooms where we had no idea what the expectation was? We often begin work on a task unaware of how good it's supposed to get. But if we can do one tiny aspect of that task really well early on, it sets the expectation level for the future. The students can then say to themselves, "Wow, the whole thing has to be that good in three months." Now they will know where you are headed. Though some may think this will cause frustration because the goal is then made so vivid, I think the opposite. I think the kids will be less frustrated with the work at hand because they will know what the finished product is to be.

I also think it works to encourage progress. Those pearls give them a feeling of accomplishment early in the process. That feeling builds as the little gems grow in number with every passing class. Accomplishment is then identified in smaller amounts early and often, rather than larger and later. They will know they have a long way to go, but that they have made real, tangible progress. Simply put, we must make something dramatically and clearly done well.

Peace

If our classes are not disciplined and quiet, nothing can get done. I believe it's that simple. That peace is essential to our success and our enjoyment of every class, but far more important, it is essential to our students' success and enjoyment of every class. I once watched a class during which the students were allowed to be free and talkative. The students were so disruptively talkative that the teacher had to yell to be heard. With that, the students yelled louder. The teacher then had to curse to be noticed. This chaotic dueling went on and escalated with every passing moment. When we talked about it, I calmly said, "What's next?" He said, "What do you mean?" I said, "All I can think of is an air-horn, and the problem with that is that once it doesn't work anymore, there is nothing left. They love pushing your buttons." They could sit back and sadly think, "How cool is it that we can get our teacher to stand there and curse out loud at us?"

He came to realize that if he really wanted to gain control, he would have to start using a series of techniques to hold a firm, disciplined and quiet class. If he stopped the screaming match with them it would burst their bubble. It would no longer be fun to get a rise out of the teacher, and they eventually would get down to work. I'm not saying we shouldn't have student interaction or that we need to be mean or so strict that there is no enjoyment, but we need to create a disciplined environment. Someone has to maintain order. I always ask people to remember that the same six letters spell the words *listen* and *silent*. I don't believe that is a coincidence! If they are not silent, they cannot listen.

Pace

I believe in a very fast pace. I sometimes like to get to the point where I know people are staying awake just to try to see if they can understand what's coming out of my mouth, and keep up with me. I also think we need lots of variations in pace as well as volume, timbre, speed, inflection, pauses, silence and accentuation. I have worked over the years to develop a generally fast pace because as a student I always found that I paid attention in class more and the time went by faster. At the end of a fast-paced class often I would think, "It's over already?" Whereas classes with a slow pace brought on almost continuous glances at my watch followed by a deep and mournful sigh. I think a fast pace with almost schizophrenic variation prevents the latter. If that is not part of your nature, that's fine. Some of the best teachers I know have a steady, calm, slow and meditative pace. However, if you are searching for ways to enliven your classroom, keep your meditative pace, but every couple of minutes add bursts of invigorated, vibrant and almost frenetic pace. *Change* in pace is even more important than trying for a *fast* pace.

Perceive

We need to become better aware of problems. We must work to sense frustration more attentively, assess errors faster, observe problems more accurately. We need to watch kids more so we can defuse discipline problems before they spread, or note when someone's lost. Simply, we must be more aware of what's going on in front of us. What's happening in our classroom? Is Susan crying? Why? Has Sam stopped writing? Is Stephanie bored because she finished so quickly? Is David using the correct worksheet? Can Mike see me with that file cabinet blocking his view? We need to observe what is *really* happening, rather than what we want to see and hear. We also can't be so preoccupied with certain students or certain places in the room that we don't perceive the big picture.

Pinpoint

Isolate the material you are going to teach. Break learning and growth down into very small steps. Teaching, or maybe

more precisely, learning, is the supreme example to me of
the adage that every long journey is made up of thousands
of single steps. The more isolated each hurdle is, the more
possible and less frustrating the process.

Polish

Years ago on my university's campus we had Shari Lewis as
a commencement speaker for the College of Education. I
might add that I was puzzled about her being chosen for
this accolade which included receiving an honorary doctor-
ate. I was taken by the non-academic nature of what she did.
After all, she was a puppeteer and television personality. All
I could think of was her little Lamb Chop wearing a cap and
gown! At the ceremony she stood to give her speech. She
started speaking, and within ten seconds, the thousands in
attendance collectively dropped their jaws. We sat mesmerized, listening to the most remarkable speaker many of us
had ever heard. During the speech she discussed the great
teachers in her life. I must hasten to mention that after the
speech I ran home and told my older sister, a gifted early
childhood education specialist, about the speech. I said,
"Ann, I just heard the most fabulous speech." She asked
by whom, to which I replied, "Shari Lewis." She quickly
responded, "Well of course, she's wonderful. You didn't
know that?" Then without missing a beat, put as only an
older sister could, she said, "Boy, you're dumber than I
thought you were!" Indeed. The following is quoted from
the marvelous Shari Lewis, whose passing was far too soon.

   She said that one of the most influential people in her
life was a Roshi, a Zen Buddhist teacher, who said, teachers:

"Concentrate on polishing your own lantern so that others may follow its light." I listened to those words, and I was changed. How many people don't do anything for themselves once they start teaching? We must continue to grow as teachers, learners and human beings. Whether it's that we continue to learn our chosen subject, study a new language, read a book, attend a conference, take classes or go to museums, we must constantly make a lifelong process of getting better at our profession. Have you ever finished reading a book one night and noticed that the next morning you had a much better class? Even if the book had nothing to do with what you were teaching? And if it was related to what you were teaching, for the next week you were about the best teacher you ever were, and then it starts to wear off. It's true. I remember the day I finished William Mitchell's exhilarating book *The Power of Positive Students*. It was a buzz I kept for three months. If we continue to get better at what we do and enjoy it even more, then our students will grow more as well, just from the glow of how much we love what we do and how excited we are to share it. Another way of saying the same thing comes from a quote by John Cotton Dana given to me by a teacher after a session I presented: "Who dares to teach must never cease to learn."

Precise

We need to be precise as to what's wrong, what we want, and what our students can do to get there. Specific information they can act on. My favorite story to illustrate this idea is attributed to Sir Thomas Beecham; however, I have heard the same story attributed to half of the conductors

in the world. It is about the player who came up to him
at rehearsal and said, "Maestro, I would like to talk to you
about rehearsal letter F in the Brahms." In a flash the Maestro screamed, "F...(long pause)...F...(longer pause)...F is
everyman. It is the world awakening, it is the essence of all
beings at one with each other, it is the soul of our collective
destiny...ah F." At which time the player looked at him and
said, "Yeah, that's great, now you want that thing loud or
soft?" It's so true. Sometimes we get so carried away that the
information we give isn't precise enough to mean anything
to anyone else. We can't be so subjective as to be meaningless. I'm certainly not saying we can't be illustrative in our
speech, and I'm as big a fan of metaphor as anyone, but at a
certain point it becomes obtuse.

Positive

We have to reinforce positive behavior all the time! Not just
sometimes, all the time. I'm a firm believer that the greater
the teacher, the more he or she uses that "gold standard" of
education. Not only does it allow us to attend to the basic
human desire to be praised, but also it allows us to do it in
a way that doesn't compromise our value system. We don't
have to look at a classroom full of students doing poorly
on an assignment and tell them they are doing wonder-
fully. They're not, and they know it. If we told them that,
it would only serve to tell them we won't be truthful about
their progress or quality. But we can always find things to
be positive about, or more specifically, ways to reinforce
positive steps toward progress. Statements about wonderful posture, good penmanship, interesting ideas, creative

thinking, exciting imagination, excellent focus, outstanding punctuation or exceptional effort.

We must truthfully praise those things done *truly* well. But equally important is to acknowledge *progress* in any area, without lying to them. Kids know when they are doing poorly, but reinforcing positive behaviors and actions moves them along the achievement path.

We have to be a positive spirit. To again paraphrase Virgil, we must always remember the simple phrase: They can who believe they can. If you convince your freshman English class they can write that essay, they *can* write that essay. If you convince them you don't believe it's possible, they won't. Haim Ginott put it so very well when he said, "I've come to the frightening conclusion that I am the decisive element in the classroom. It is my personal approach that creates the climate. It is my daily mood that makes the weather. As a teacher I possess a tremendous power to make a child's life miserable or joyous. I can be a tool of torture or an instrument of inspiration." Quite possibly, those are some of the best words to live by I've ever come across.

Pleasant

Do we create an environment that is pleasant? Is it safe and comfortable? Do our students have moments of success? Are they free to feel emotions or dream lofty dreams without fear of ridicule? Do the students sense they can try, confident in the knowledge they will be told when it is wrong, but that they will be praised when it is correct? Now before you roll your eyes, I think moments where students are on the edges of their chairs are wonderful and healthy, but there have to be many moments we create where students can't help but leave our classrooms thinking their time with us was pleasant.

Pleasurable

Do *you* have fun in class? Do *they* have fun in class? I'm convinced that if the first is true, the second will be too. There are a lot of times when my students tell me that I "ought to get a life." I think it's because I seem to have a lot of fun in my classroom. I have a ball. I do, I really do. To me it's real serious business. I eat it, breathe it, and sleep it. I love it. They are some of the most earnest moments in my life. That doesn't mean it's not fun. I want my students to see that hard work can be very enjoyable and that I really enjoy teaching and learning, not by my telling them so, but by my living it.

Pause

Breaks from rigorous work are necessary. Intensity is great, I'm a firm believer in it, but there have to be breaks from it. It doesn't matter whether it's a story, a joke, a silence, a review, as long as there are breaks from the monotony and redundancy of relentless, intense work. My favorite story about the need for a break of this kind comes from a time I was working with a very large all-state band. One hundred sixty-one of us were packed into a classroom which eventually grew to be hotter than the surface of the sun. On the side of the room were several sets of double doors leading outside. We kept them open at all times. For three days they rehearsed with incredible focus while being as quiet and behaved as any group in history.

During some very demanding work at the morning rehearsal of the third day, all of a sudden there was a giant, violent crack of lightning and thunder instantly followed by a torrential downpour. As I continued to teach, the students started to laugh. They held it in until it boiled over and spread from student to student like a virus. Within a flash they were all laughing uncontrollably. At that moment I had to make a decision as to what to do. My first thought, I must admit, was, "These kids have been so well behaved for three days, and now they are going to sit there and laugh!" Then I realized they had been working so intensely that they obviously needed it. They needed to collectively "lose it." By then the virus had gotten to me. It was so infectious that people were falling over and holding their sides. I was laughing so hard that I pulled a muscle in my ribcage. After a minute or two, as the laughter had simmered down to a dull, out-of-breath sighing, I asked them what we were laughing at. Through tears of laughter they answered, "We have no idea!" After about another twenty seconds, the laughter stopped as fast as it started, and we went right back to work. The rest of that rehearsal was probably our best. They needed it. Why? I have no idea.

People who watch me teach must wonder why anyone who tells jokes as poorly as I do would ever tell a joke in public. Or why I tell my dumb stories or anecdotes. They aren't very good, but they are designed to give that momentary pause when needed. When I have pressed them as far as I think I can press them, I will often back away for a minute and let them laugh, or giggle, or sit quietly, or make fun of one of my stupid jokes.

Pass

There will always be those times when we have to just "let go." And on those occasions, we have to change our course to steer away from the arduous challenges of the "rapids" to find enjoyment, fulfillment and unnoticed beauty in the "calm waters" we are in now. Knowing full well that tomorrow, or the tomorrow after that will be a better day to head straight into those rapids. At those times when we decide it isn't going to happen, we need to be willing to simply *pass*. There's always tomorrow or next week. If it's the rainy day before Thanksgiving vacation and it's not happening, let it go. Because we all know that if we push too hard at the wrong time, the damage done could take us three weeks to undo. Just let it go. I'm not saying to let chaos run rampant, but we may need to back off some on our expectations for that session. On those days, playing a game as a way of reviewing facts already learned or doing some kind of creative activity to use old material in new ways may be wonderful opportunities found.

People

No matter what we do in classes, or how we do it, we have to always remember they're people. They may be young or old. They may be seasoned or inexperienced. They may be sharp as a tack or need a bit more time. But they are people. They don't belong to us. Nor will they stay with us. We just have to make certain they will be all the better for the time we share together as human beings. There is a time when what we know matters little, who we have been is meaningless, what we have accomplished is insignificant and what talents we possess are unimportant. That time is when we are looking at those faces in every class. Those human beings who have entrusted themselves to us. I believe they are much less concerned about our past accolades than they are about whether we care about them. I'm certainly not saying we have to be warm and fuzzy all the time, or that they shouldn't know when we are displeased, but we need to respect them as we wish them to respect us.

Pep Talk

We always need to bolster their confidence. We need to be the one to instill determination. We have to be the one to build their enthusiasm. They can't always do it themselves. We have to help them do it. We must be the catalyst. They can come on board once we have the train moving. But they need our help. Often I wonder if we teachers weren't all cheerleaders in another life. We all know sometimes that's what it takes.

Picture

We can't work so much on detail that we forget to put what is learned in context. Often we work so hard on teaching specific things, the parts that make the whole, that the casualty of our focused teaching is perspective, the big picture as a whole. The perspective to know such things as how and when to use what's been learned, where it came from and to where it leads.

I learned this best from my father who loved to fly small airplanes. He was a wonderful pilot. I had always wanted to get my license. When I started training, I didn't tell him. I wanted to surprise him. So after I got my license, I called him from my home in Connecticut and asked him to meet me for lunch at the North Philadelphia Airport. That Saturday, with my dad on the field, I flew in with the best landing of my life. I then pulled the plane over to the parking area from where my dad was proudly watching. I walked over to get a great big congratulatory hug. Then, after we discussed his surprise, we went into the airport for lunch. After lunch, we went to the airplane to take a ride. He asked whether I wanted to do the preflight inspection or should he. I confidently said that I would. In an effort to convince my dad, who was the best pilot I had ever known, that I really knew what I was doing, I proceeded to give that airplane the most thorough, detailed and focused preflight in the history of aviation.

I checked every screw. I knew every rivet by name. I'm pretty convinced I could have given you the social security number of the person who tightened every bolt and what he ate for breakfast on the day he did it! I checked every detail as if with a magnifying glass. My father stood and watched every moment. At the end, I called over to him and said, "All done, let's go." His response: "Hell no, I'm not getting in that deathtrap!" He went on to say that I wasn't done. I stood there trying to figure out what I had missed. What detail had I neglected? He then walked away from the plane and stood looking at its nose. I walked over and stood next to him. He then asked if I was "looking at the plane." I said, "Yes." He asked if I was "really looking at the whole airplane." I said, "Yes." He then said, "Now you're done."

As we walked to the plane, I asked him to explain the lesson he undoubtedly was trying to teach me. He feared I was so preoccupied by the minutia of the details, looking in such a myopic way, that I would miss the big picture: the bent wing or leak on the ground, only seen with the perspective provided by distance. He said, "You were so worried about the rivets and screws that it could have been the wrong airplane and you wouldn't have noticed it."

So for us, we always need to look at the big picture of what's being learned. When studying a doctrine, event, person or idea, it is our students having the perspective to understand the people who created that doctrine, to know what caused that event in history, to comprehend the context of educational content, and to grasp the steps which led to the development of an idea which matter greatly. Surely knowledge is best viewed with that perspective, the perspective of the big picture. Dad would like that.

Past

Make sure that we always review what has been learned. I constantly remind myself of the phenomenal truth found in the phrase, "We need be taught much less than we need be reminded."

Push

We always have to press them to be ever better. Constantly raising the bar. They need to know that the second they get over the bar, it is instantly three inches higher. The expectation is that they will constantly try their hardest to improve bit by bit. The bits may be small, but always better. The story I tell every ensemble with which I have ever worked is about a time I was conducting in a very poor region of this country. It was one of the poorest areas I had ever been in. I was rehearsing in the "cafe-gymna-bandroom-natorium," which was affectionately called "the room." It was the only large room they had which I came to find out was used for every large event in the region. We spent several days working very hard. They were wonderful students and played incredibly well. They were, however, from humble means. They were playing on instruments being held together with duct tape that I would have made into a planter years before. They had little, if one measures by earthly possessions. Just before the concert, they taught me what *they had* that was far greater. I was told to wait in the hall outside of the cafe-gymna-bandroom-natorium to be announced for the start of the performance.

I stood quietly listening to my introduction. As I did, I happened to look up above the door leading into the room and saw a small wooden plaque where someone had etched in the following words with a pen: "Today I will give everything I have, for anything I keep I will have lost forever." I stood there as tears filled my eyes. I heard my name announced. I heard the applause, but I couldn't move. Finally, my host came over to the door and asked if I was ready. Seeing the tears, he asked if I was okay. I replied that I just needed a minute. I was absolutely dumbfounded. Those people had the integrity, work ethic, and dedication to publicly state they weren't going to waste one minute. It wasn't about doing their best for the big game, the big vote, the big test or the big performance, it was about doing their best every time they entered that room, no matter what they were doing. They realized that any opportunity they had, but missed, to make it better, was lost forever.

I try to think of that every time I walk into a class thinking it's just going to be a class. It isn't just the next forty-five minutes. It is the only time those forty-five minutes will exist. Those dedicated and talented students and teachers knew. They taught me more that day than they ever could have known. As W. Somerset Maugham reminds us, "It is a funny thing about life: If you refuse to accept anything but the best, you often get it."

Persevere

We must continue the course no matter what. No matter the difficulty. No matter the opposition. No matter the frustration. We can't get discouraged. I'm not saying that we have to be so rigid with our plans as not to take those unexpected detours of creative teaching which are often our best moments, or at times we can't take that "pass" on our goal for the day. I'm talking about the big picture. The path you want students to take to get to where you know you are going. That place where you can step back, view what they have achieved, realize what *you* have given them, realize what *they* have given you, and more important realize what they have given *themselves*. It will happen. They will get there. It may take a bit longer than any of us would like, but if we stay the course, it is going to happen. Marilyn vos Savant was so very correct when she said, "Being defeated is only a temporary condition, giving up is what makes it permanent."

Praise

We all know we must constantly reward achievement. Human nature being what it is, we all want that pat on the back. The problem we often find ourselves in is that we either have to wait until something is really great to reward it, or we have to lie and say it is great when it isn't. If we wait until something is perfect, we often will be praising our students sometime in the next millennium. If we lie, they will probably know it and then ignore all future praise, assuming it too is a lie, or they will believe us and develop such low expectations that we will never convince them of the goals ahead. The only way out is to break our achievement objectives into such small amounts — such tiny steps — as to allow them to achieve great results on a regular basis. That gives us the opportunity to truthfully and frequently praise real results.

But how do we instill a sense of appreciation and reward for results that are getting better, but are still not very good? I used to teach with a wonderful gentleman who always reminded his education students to "praise approximation." I hated that thought! I wrestled with that sentiment in my mind until I was exhausted. It truly bothered me. Then I realized our disagreement was semantic in nature. I took the word "praise" in his mantra to mean that if the achievement was even approximately correct we should tell them it was great. What he meant was that we have to acknowledge and reward the fact that the results are getting ever closer to the goal. Quite simply we have to be encouraging along the way rather than wait until a goal is truly *reached*. Just remember that the same letters that make the word *praise* are used to make the word *aspire*. If we don't praise them, they will not aspire. We don't have to wait until it's perfect to help them know it's getting better.

Pride

They need to be proud of their accomplishments from your praising them, and from their sensing their success. They need to know when you are happy and pleased with their progress or achievements. True, our goal should be that they sense personal fulfillment from within; however, we have to show them how proud we are of them along the way. Adapting that well-known maxim, "We must help them to take pride in how far they have come, and to have faith in how far they can go."

Plant

You know what we are? We're farmers. We plant seeds. We plant seeds that we may never see come to complete fruition. That's what we do. It is sometimes hard to remember that. We can't get frustrated or try to tackle too much now because we are planting seeds for the next month, the next year, the next generation, for time to come. Don't think that just because they "didn't get it" now, they won't someday "get it." You may be wondering why I chose to use the word plant in this chapter rather than the word patience. I did so because to me, planting, with the above connotation, is the ultimate in patience. I often think of patience as being sought for the moment, as opposed to planting, which implies holding one's patience for a very long germination.

Perspective

Keep it all in perspective: the moment, the class and the year. Remember what's really important: that they love and appreciate learning, themselves and their world. With your guidance, patience and example, they will.

Productive

Do *you* and do *they* feel the goals with which we started this chapter have been accomplished? Because if you don't, or they don't, something is wrong in the process.

Passion

We have to have and to show this most contagious of things called passion. Jim Elliot once wrote, "He is no fool who gives what he cannot keep to gain what he cannot lose." You can give as much passion about teaching, about learning, about life, about your subject matter as you want and it will never deplete your supply, for you were not destined to keep that. The joy of their experiencing that passion, however, can never be taken away. The smiles on their faces, the tears in their eyes, when you know they have experienced joy, is a gift for all time that you can never lose.

Potential

Never underestimate their potential or your potential. As the saying goes, "Kids can do anything, we just have to show them how." According to Anatole France, "To accomplish great things, we must not only act, but also dream; not only plan, but also believe." We can follow the advice of the remarkable sentiment: "To achieve all that is possible, we must attempt the impossible. To be as much as we can be, we must dream of being more."

Powerful

Never lose sight of the power of what we do. It never ceases to amaze me how overwhelming it is. We help people expand their knowledge, express their emotions, cherish their curiosity and challenge their views. That is our job. We teach people to learn. We teach people to cry. We help people to experience heights of excitement they have never known. We have the ability to touch people's minds as much as their souls. We can change their lives.

Years ago, I was given a poem by a student. As I read her words, tears streamed down my face. The poem hangs framed on the wall in my office. It is positioned so that all I have to do when I get frustrated and decide I should give up is to turn around and it is right at eye level staring at me. Suffice it to say it seems I read it about ten times a day! It has gotten me through the best and worst of times. It is not coincidence that you will notice many of her words present in the preceding pages.

Though it was given to me, it is really a gift meant for all teachers. I just happen to be the caretaker. All of your students have either said or thought the same things about you. They might not have taken the time to write them down, or they may be too shy to show them to you if they had, but this is what every single student in your classes

thinks, has thought and will think. This is how important
what you do is in the life of a child. Even if they don't know
these words, this is what they want to say to you:

> "I catch your eye
> and hold it,
> hold it for an eternity.
> Your eyes
>   scream with excitement,
>   anger,
>   pride,
>   satisfaction,
>   exhilaration.
> Your eyes
>   speak of love,
>   concern,
>   understanding.
> Your eyes
>   cry with a strong desire,
>   a desperate yearning,
>   to help us reach
>   our full potentials,
>   our goals.
> You care —
>   I can see it in your eyes."

The next time you get frustrated or wonder what this is
all really about, remember that your students are looking
right at your eyes and into your heart and soul. ▨

FROM MUDDY WATERS

I had a dream once that I was conducting a fifth-grade beginning band. It was our first rehearsal. As I started to conduct, they began to play a remarkably difficult piece of music by composer David Holsinger entitled *To Tame the Perilous Skies*. And let me tell you, they didn't just "play" it, they performed it magnificently. It was truly amazing. It was also a dream. Now there was some truth to my dream. I had worked with a fifth-grade band earlier that day. They truly needed to be "tamed," and there was much in that rehearsal which sounded quite "perilous." However, that is where the similarities stopped.

Don't we all wish we could teach classrooms full of students who have achieved well beyond their years and are truly gifted learners? Yes, maybe deep down we might, but every teacher knows our true calling is to take students from where they are and move them to where we know they can go. Wherever they may be when we get them, we must nurture and encourage each of them to "Bloom where you are planted." Is it easy? Of course not. But our challenge is to follow the admonition of Theodore Roosevelt: "Do what you can, with what you have, where you are."

We do that every day, knowing that what we do and how we do it will impact our students far more powerfully than any knowledge or skill. Our teaching is more far-reaching, influential and enduring than we can imagine. Every day is filled with frustrations, but every day is also filled with promise: not just for what we will teach our students, but also for how we will impact their lives. Each time we stand in front of them, we must remember Graham Greene's words: "There is always one moment in childhood when the door opens and lets the future in." That is the profound power of what we do. We can make *that moment* for each of our students. A moment they may not even realize for years, when, in the middle of a class, *we* opened a door and helped them to let their future in.

Sometimes, as we all know, it is difficult to keep that in mind. How easy it is to be discouraged by the fundamental skills or past achievements of our students. How easy it is to get frustrated with their levels of preparation from the past, which can weigh heavily on our hopes for their futures. And though the knowledge and abilities of those same students may someday be as flawless as a crystal clear spring-fed stream, during those frustrating times they appear to be more like a muddy swamp. Well, when you see those muddy waters, think of the wonderful Zen teaching which reminds us that the amazingly exquisite lotus flower grows only in swamps or marshes, rising out of those muddy waters to bloom with almost unimaginable beauty.

We must reach down to where our students are, no matter how "muddy" that is, and help them to bloom. Knowing, as John Andrew Holmes observed, "There is no exercise better for the heart than reaching down and lifting people

up." That's the funny thing about teachers. We have the
ability to see the work of any student, no matter how disap-
pointing, and get excited at the thought of transforming
those abilities into something grand. Where the average
human being would run away from that challenge, we savor
that opportunity.

Maybe it's for the same reasons some people see an
empty jar as trash, while others see it as a pencil holder,
vase or penny bank. Vision: the ability to see what is invisible. Better still, being able to see something *that is* as what
it *can be*. Pablo Picasso stated, "Some painters transform the
sun into a yellow spot, others transform a yellow spot into
the sun." We take the "yellow spots" that are our students
and help them to become their best "sun." Picasso would
have made a great teacher!

We all know it's easier said than done. We all know it
is never-ending work. But we also know it is our mission,
our calling and a joy we wouldn't trade for anything. Will
you encounter those who say it's futile or impossible? Sure,
and when you do, just think to yourself, "People who say it
cannot be done should not interrupt those who are doing
it." So take that empty jar, fill it with yellow paint and
transform that spot into the sun. Let it shine down its light
on those muddy waters, and help a beautiful lotus flower to
emerge from that swamp for all to see.

THE VIEW FROM THE MOUNTAINTOP

There I sat, looking at my computer screen while tears came down my face. I had just received an email from one of my students. In that, her senior year, she was an amazing student in every way. I will never forget the words she wrote: "I need to thank you for never allowing me to be satisfied with less than what I am capable of; for never allowing me to cheat myself out of knowing exactly what my personal best is; and for keeping me reminded of why I chose this path in the first place."

That email was even more special than you might think; let me try to explain why by going back in time three years before it arrived. I can remember as if it were yesterday having that same young lady, then a freshman, in my class. I can flash back to times where I was frustrated to say the least. Quite frankly, early on, there were moments when it was a good thing I had no hair, because I would have pulled it out.

Deep down I knew she wanted to be a fine student. The truth is she motivated herself; I only watched and smiled.

But I did try to push her ever further and to encourage her to believe in the power of her dreams. And day by day, with hard work, dedication and commitment, she surpassed even my wildest dreams in a precious few years.

In our own way, we each help our students to progress. My goal has always been that what *they now know* is what *they once never imagined*. Striving for ever-higher goals is like taking in the view of a mountaintop from the ground below. When you're standing at the foot of a mountain, the only view is that peak you are trying to reach. It seems to be the only goal, so we work hard to get there. Only after we reach that summit do we see the top of an even higher mountain that now seems to have the highest peak. We work to get to that zenith, only to see one still higher. The funny thing is at the base of any mountain, its peak seems to be the loftiest height. It is *only* the view from the mountaintop that allows us to see the next even-higher place.

We must remember—and our students must learn the lesson—that we can never see what goals lie ahead. We can only work to reach our goals one summit at a time, knowing all the while we will go even farther than we can now fathom. How high will we, or our students, eventually reach? Who knows? As Pumbaa the lovable warthog queried in the movie *Lion King* 1½, "But, if you always go beyond what you see, how do you know when you're there?" You don't! However, as long as we all enjoy the journey, it will be worth every moment of it. We each strive for the best from ourselves and our students: one step at a time; one hill at a time; one mountaintop at a time.

I hope we can all push our students, and ourselves, never to settle for getting to the top of one mountain, to always look for the next peak. The trick is to remember to enjoy the view from the top of even the smallest hill and savor the beauty of that success. I share that email with you because it is what each of your students wants to say to you. The next time you look into the eyes of your students, know they thank you for never allowing them to be satisfied with less than what *they* are capable of; for never allowing them to cheat themselves out of knowing exactly what *their* personal bests are. They may rarely express it, but know they will *always* appreciate it.

FAILURE IS
OPPORTUNITY
TURNED UPSIDE
DOWN

One evening, while in Richmond, Virginia, I was driving with several teachers on our way to dinner. We were trying to find a restaurant in a congested part of town. As we got close to the restaurant, one gentleman said, "It's your next left turn." There was only one problem: a sign that said, "No Left Turn." The car filled with some tension as it seemed the sign would make our route to the restaurant impossible. At that moment, one teacher said, "Well, as one of my grade school teachers always said, 'Two wrongs don't make a right, but three rights make a left.'"

Not being the sharpest knife in the drawer, I sat there puzzled as I processed his words, drawing a sketch in my mind. And sure enough, he was *right*, well, correct. Three rights do make a left. What a perfect metaphor for failure.

On the surface, we failed at making our needed left turn. However, our driver used that *opportunity* to *succeed* by putting us on a different path. One, I might add, that gave me the chance to see even more of the landmarks of that beautiful city. He didn't think he had failed, he didn't give up, he didn't panic. He saw that sign as a result, not a failure. He saw possibility and opportunity in finding a different way to achieve our goal.

Those words brilliantly describe how each of us, and our students, have choices every time we encounter what might be seen as failure.

What is Failure?

Truly, failure is a state of mind. It is all in how we see each of our attempts at something. Is each of them a negative event we dread, or is it just an outcome? As Wayne Dyer wrote, "You can never fail, you just produce results." How much easier it is for us to handle times when things don't happen the way we wish, when we view them simply as the result of what we did.

Give Yourself Permission to Fail

How many times have we been stopped by fear of failing? That fear can be powerful. And I think the younger the person the worse that fear is perceived. The first step in changing our students' attitudes about failure is simply convincing them it is okay to fail, that failing is simply one *possible* result of trying, but undoubtedly a *necessary* step in succeeding. As

Marva Collins said, "If you can't make a mistake, you can't make anything." In the words of my dear friend Tim Lautzenheiser, "A mistake is at least evidence that someone tried to do something."

One of the greatest sentiments about giving oneself permission to fail comes from Samuel Beckett: "Ever tried. Ever failed. No matter. Try again. Fail again. Fail better." What a remarkable concept: *failing better*. How free is one who not only can embrace failure as *necessary*, but has given oneself permission not just to fail, but to fail better the next time?

Failure is Knowledge

Oscar Wilde said, "Experience is the name everyone gives to their mistakes." Those results we call failures are actually great sources of important data. With a healthy dose of reflection, each time we "fail" we become armed with valuable information that will make our next attempt more informed. Basically, failure is knowledge and knowledge is power. As Thomas Edison so eloquently stated, "I have not failed. I've just found 10,000 ways that won't work."

Every Failure is an Opportunity

I know it seems like optimism gone wild, but it's true. Each time we fail we are given a chance, a chance to try again, now far more knowledgeable about what works and what doesn't work. As Henry Ford perfectly concluded, "Failure is the opportunity to begin again, more intelligently."

Failure Might Require Change

Often we need only to be receptive to the thought that failure might require change and to be willing to look at the task at hand with different eyes. In that way, we will heed the warning of Helen Keller: "When one door of happiness closes, another opens; but often we look so long at the closed door that we do not see the one which has been opened for us." Focusing over and over on the same approach for the same goal may just make us spin our wheels with great effort yet little reward. More often than not it is simply having the ability to "Follow success with success; follow failure with change."

Failure as a Challenge

Let's say we have achieved a specific goal and are now able to do what we set out to accomplish. We succeeded. But what happens when we try that same ability in a more difficult setting — raising the bar, if you will — and we fail? That failure has given us the chance to become better at what we do by challenging our abilities. Doing a task or technique is good. Doing that same thing in a more demanding situation is better. Remember the wonderful African proverb that reminds us, "Smooth seas do not make skillful sailors." Once we learn to sail, we only get better by challenging ourselves with ever more choppy seas.

Failure Can Be Success

The astounding Heraclitus offered this wisdom: "When there is no sun, we can see the evening stars." Every time I think of that statement I get chills. It is as true as it is powerful. Our goal may be to see the beautiful mountains or breathtaking flowers of life. A terrific goal. But if the sun goes down, leaving us in darkness, we will fail. Often we will then expend enormous amounts of energy bemoaning the darkness and cursing our failure. However, it is only that darkness — the darkness that made us fail — that can offer us the beauty of the night sky.

If we had spent all of our efforts trying to change or "fix" the darkness, we would never have had the opportunity to see the majesty of the evening stars. True, we might just stumble upon those moments by accident, but an open mind and a willingness to look beyond and around the failure may yield growth and beauty more marvelous than we ever imagined. Failure is many things, *not* all of which are bad; in fact, viewed correctly, failure can be a gift in disguise.

Failure is a Choice

Every time we don't succeed, or hit that "No Left Turn" sign, each of us — and each of our students — is faced with a decision. Do we give up or do we persevere? When we try to do something new or more difficult we often just can't make that "left turn." But is that a reason to give up? No; we might just have to change those "left turns" we want to make in life into "three right turns" in order to get where we want to go. Remember, "No one is a failure who keeps trying."

It is sad to come to understand that "Many of life's failures," as Thomas Edison reminds us, "are experienced by people who did not realize how close they were to success when they gave up." Those people simply didn't keep in mind those four Latin words which remind us: *Nemo nisi intus superatus.* ("You only get beaten from within.")

We can help our students to view failure as an outcome rather than a bad event, as an opportunity to find another way, as a chance to grow and learn, and to think around obstacles or failures. But of greater importance, we must teach them never to give up. Our students must come to learn, as the following anonymous poem asserts, the only thing which can stop them — is them. So maybe failure is quite simply opportunity turned upside down.

Don't Quit

When things go wrong as they sometimes will;
When the road you're trudging seems all uphill;
When the funds are low, and the debts are high
And you want to smile but have to sigh;
When care is pressing you down a bit –
Rest if you must, but do not quit.

Success is failure turned inside out;
The silver tint of the clouds of doubt;
And you can never tell how close you are
It may be near when it seems so far;
So stick to the fight when you're hardest hit –
It's when things go wrong that you must not quit.

"WITHOUT YOU, THERE NEVER WOULD HAVE BEEN A JOURNEY"

M any years ago I was sitting at the desk in my office. I was tired and a bit frustrated. I had lost a few then-recent battles, wasn't really sure I was getting my message across to my students and had begun to feel more and more gloomy. As my son Matthew once wisely philosophized at the ripe old age of nine, "I had too much on my plate, and was too tired to chew."

As I sat there staring at the wall in front of my desk, a student walked by my open door, peered in and saw me looking less than zippy. She said hello and asked if I was okay. In that I responded with a pretty dull, "sure," she perceptively said I looked tired and low and asked me what was wrong.

Her next words, however, shook me to the core, when she asked, "Has your star burned out?" I puzzled for a moment, then asked her what she meant. She went on to describe how my sparkle seemed faded. At that moment, I was as dumbstruck as *she* was correct. After she left, I couldn't stop thinking about what she had said. I couldn't stop thinking of how right she was. My star *had* certainly become dull.

A few days later, she came back to see me. She was carrying a box and an envelope, which she quietly presented to me. Her only instructions were to read the letter before opening the box. And oh what a letter it was. In it she described her journey as a student, and thanked me for being a part of that path. Through her words I realized, more than ever before, how important the glow of our excitement and enthusiasm can be to our students. And that we can never allow anything to stand in the way of it shining light on the path that is the journey of learning. She ended her letter—this magnificent letter—with nine words I will never forget, nine words that centered my focus, nine words that strengthened my resolve, nine words I will spend the rest of my life trying to deserve. "Just remember," she wrote, "without you, there never would have been a journey."

Utterly speechless, almost trembling at the thought of what she had written, I opened the box. There I saw a beautiful, shining, silver paperweight in the shape of a perfect five-point star. On it were engraved those nine amazing words. Those nine words that took my breath away.

The problem was that I forgot. I forgot how important what we do, how we do it, and who we are, can be. I forgot sometimes we lose those battles but win a much more important war. I forgot the insight of Cullen Hightower who declared, "A true measure of your worth includes all the benefits others have gained from your success." I forgot the wisdom of Benjamin Disraeli who proclaimed, "The greatest good you can do for another is not just to share your riches but to reveal to him his own." I forgot the perceptiveness of Sir Winston Churchill who affirmed, "We make a living by what we get, we make a life by what we give." I forgot the brilliance of Galileo who advised, "You cannot teach a man anything, you can only help him discover it within himself." I forgot my purpose — my *true* purpose — best described in the wonderful Irish proverb: "The tree remains, but not the hand that planted it."

I forgot. I simply forgot. But all at once, holding that star, the shining light of that student — that extraordinary student — helped me to remember the joy of teaching, the impact of teaching and the responsibility of teaching. She reminded me of the profound honor it is to help young people discover that learning is not a destination, but a journey, an incredibly wonderful journey to be devoured, savored and cherished. More significant, she reminded me of just how lucky we are to get to share that journey with all those whom we teach.

Are there still those days I can feel my star fading? Absolutely. But then I look at my paperweight star and remember. I remember the remarkable kindness of an equally remarkable student. I remember the faces of those I have had the privilege to teach. I remember their smiles, their tears, their frustrations, their successes. But mostly I remember the importance, the incredible importance of what we do.

So the next time you feel your star begin to fade, look deeper into your students' eyes and remember those words — those nine simple words. Remember your purpose. Remember *what you are* in the lives of your students. Remember their faces. But above all else, remember that "Without *you*, there never would have been a journey." A precious journey indeed. Remember.

WORRY

I don't like to worry, though Lord knows I do more than my fair share of it. For certain aspects of my life I have elevated worrying to an art form. You might say that if worrying became an Olympic sport I would be a gold-medal winner with few contenders in my league. But as much as I worry about most everything in life, I almost never worry about teaching classes. Odd, isn't it? One would think those sessions would be the source of many worries, but strangely they are not. Why? It doesn't make any sense.

I don't know about you, but I worry about what I can't control: that for which I feel helpless. I believe that if we have prepared as much as we could, we shouldn't be worried. We have done all we could. It's when we haven't prepared as well as possible that worry has every right to take hold of us. If we walk into class with a firm knowledge of our material and a detailed lesson plan, what is there to worry *about*? We have done everything possible to ensure success. That is also a lesson I try to pass along to students. Whether one is taking an exam or performing on the stage, worrying is wasted energy. Preparation is proactive energy. Once we feel we have truly prepared to our best ability, worry has no purpose. I know it's easier said than done, but it is too logical to be ignored. As my dear friend Jerry Tyson says, "Worry is only borrowing from tomorrow's problems, bringing no relief from those of today." How very true!

The illustrious Leo Buscaglia offered the same sentiment with, "Worry never robs tomorrow of its sorrow, it only saps today of its joy." But my favorite thought regarding the foolishness of spending today worrying about tomorrow was given to me by my then seven-year-old son Matthew, quoting a "SpongeBob SquarePants" cartoon in which Mr. Krabs ended an argument with the undeniable words: "What is today but yesterday's tomorrow?" Just remember that today is the tomorrow you worried about yesterday!

If we are ill-prepared, causing us to worry, we won't enjoy our teaching, our students or the precious time we have with them. Worrying is no fun. It eats us alive, ages us and tends to make us negative and surly. Worry predisposes us to being in a defensive, survival mode rather than an optimistic, offensive posture. The confidence fueled by preparation leads us to be receptive and eager about the road ahead rather than to be worried about what's around the next turn. Our students will learn that valuable lesson from our example. Worry on the face or in the voice of a teacher translates to fear and trepidation for students who are looking to their teacher as a model. They may not even know what to worry about, but worry they will if that's how we condition them.

I don't like to worry and I don't like what my worrying does to my students. Knowing I have done all I can before each class prevents me from having to fret. That way I can save all that good worrying for everything else in my everyday life.

IT'S ALL IN
HOW YOU SEE IT

The bell just rang. It's now three o'clock in the afternoon. The school day has ended. As usual, before leaving for home, you have many things to do and a million thoughts running through your head: "I need to find a better way of getting my students to remember those verb tenses. What can I do to 'reach' Steve and Bill and Sue? What can I say to convince Bobby that I believe in his ability to solve those word problems in math? I need to find another science experiment to review what my kids learned today. If Fred turns in another paper with his name spelled incorrectly I'll scream. When will my students ever learn the rule for 'i before e'? Boy did Joe mess up that run-through of our class play. If I have to tell the boys in the back of my classroom to be quiet one more time! I am so tired of trying to convince my last period class of the joys of poetry. If only my school principal could understand why what I teach is so important. One more third-grade-humor joke in class and I'll die." Thoughts like those, and more than this book could contain.

Only this day is different. It is the day you retire from teaching. This day you will pack up your things, turn off the light and lock your classroom for the last time. The door will close. You will turn that key as you always have. But this time, knowing you will never return, the sound of the lock rings out like a cannon blast. At that moment, everything changes. Now, as you walk out of the building, those earlier thoughts change. They are suddenly transformed into: "I'll miss the challenge of finding a better way of getting my students to remember those verb tenses. When Steve, Bill and Sue finally 'get it' they will be unstoppable. I'll miss giving those pep talks to Bobby about how much I believe in his ability to solve those word problems in math. I just thought of the perfect science experiment to review what my kids learned today, but I'll never get to see them do it. I'll miss the chance to smile from ear to ear when Fred turns in a paper with his name spelled correctly. One more day and I could have gotten my students to learn the rule for 'i before e.' I'll miss the delight on Joe's face after the first successful run-through of our class play. I wonder what I could have done to better engage those boys in the back of my classroom. I'll miss the utter joy in the eyes of my last period class when poetry finally allows them to feel something inside themselves they didn't even know existed. I wish I had included my principal in our class project so she would have heard what I heard and saw what I saw. I'll miss the silly third-grade jokes and the chance to see those who told them turn into adults."

What changed? They are the same problems, the same students, the same classes and the same principal. What changed is our perspective. Do we now view things the

same way we did on our first day of teaching? Do you
remember the very first class you taught, the first day of
your teaching career? Do you remember how excited you
were and how much you reveled in the process of teaching?
Do you remember the thrill it gave you? Do you remember
the look on those students' faces? Do you remember the
sheer joy you felt when you realized that at last you were
indeed a teacher? Nothing has changed. Has it? Students
still need to be taught how to conjugate verbs. They still
look toward the teacher for that training. The leak in the
ceiling of your classroom is still there. You still have that
tie you had on your first day of teaching. So what changed?

When that student turns in a paper with as many tense
errors as words, we can view the glass as half empty and
think to ourselves: "I have to fix that again?" Or we can
view the same glass as half full and think: "I get the chance
to help a student learn concepts which will serve him for
the rest of his life." Simply, we must *embrace* the *opportunities*
to *teach*. We must relish the joys of the teaching, not just
the moments when something has been learned. As Hugh
Prather so aptly stated, "Happiness is a present attitude and
not a future condition."

Some of the most exceptional words I know are those
of Betty Smith, who said, "Look at everything as if you
were seeing it either for the first time or the last time. Then
your time on earth will be filled with glory." If we follow
that sage advice, we will know our time on earth as teachers will be glorious, enjoyable and empowering. The next
time you look at those students of yours, and see the "same
old problems" while sighing at the very thought of fixing
them, realize you have a choice. View those moments with

disdain and fatigue, or with excitement and enthusiasm. Just remember the words of Ashleigh Brilliant: "Strangely enough, this is the past that somebody in the future is longing to go back to."

I always try to keep in mind that touching admonition, mentioned earlier, by Herb Gardner: "You have got to own your days and name them, each one of them, every one of them, or else the years go right by and none of them belong to you." How do we "own" our days as teachers? By reveling in the opportunities to teach, savoring the chance to impact young lives and remembering the successes. Then, after the years have gone by, all of those days *will* belong to us, as will the memories of those students and what we helped them to become as people.

What you do, how you do it, and how you feel about it changes when you simply "Look at everything as if you were seeing it either for the first time or the last time." I dare say the day we lock our classroom for the last time we will remember the day we unlocked it for the first time. I hope we make all the days in between filled with the same sense of awe.

It is, quite simply, all in how we choose to see it. Maybe it comes down to following the wisdom of that renowned philosopher Ziggy, when he profoundly counseled, "You can complain because roses have thorns, or you can rejoice because thorns have roses."

"DO OR DO NOT, THERE IS NO TRY"

What a powerful phrase. Those words were spoken by that remarkable philosopher and teacher, Yoda, in the movie *Star Wars: The Empire Strikes Back*, during a scene at his home in the Dagoba System. Luke Skywalker was there to complete his training under Yoda's guidance. As the scene opens, Luke is doing a handstand. There standing on top of Luke's feet is Yoda. Luke is hard at work trying to make a large stone rise in the air, using only "the force." As Luke struggles, Yoda says to his young charge, "Use the force — yes. Now — the stone. Feel it." As Luke starts to lose control, and they begin to fall to the ground, Yoda exclaims, "Concentrate."

At that point, looking toward his X-Wing fighter stranded in the murky swamp near them, Luke sighs, "Oh no, we'll never get it out now." For in Luke's mind, the goal or only reason for doing that exercise was to right his ship. Calmly, Yoda says, "So certain are you. Always with you: it cannot be done. Hear you nothing that I say?" More concerned with the goal than the ability, Luke replies, "Master, moving stones around is one thing. This is totally different." Growing more disappointed, Yoda states, "No, no different. Only different in your mind. You must unlearn what you have learned." Reluctantly and with a defeated sound in his voice, Luke replies, "Alright, I'll give it a try."

Now more frustrated and distressed, Yoda implores, "No, try not. Do, or do not—there is no try." Aiming his hand at the X-Wing buried in the swap, Luke intensely tries to make his craft rise in the air. Slowly, it starts to ascend a bit, but then falls back to the swamp. Both student and teacher sigh. Luke sits down near Yoda, and says, "I can't, it's too big." With growing impatience, Yoda replies, "Size matters not. Look at me, judge me by my size do you, hmm? And well you should not, for my ally is the force. And a powerful ally it is. Life creates it, makes it grow. Its energy surrounds us, and binds us. Luminous beings are we, not this crude matter. You must feel the force around you. Here, between you—me—the tree, the rock, everywhere, yes even between land and the ship." Luke, now completely frustrated, responds by saying, "You want the impossible." With that said, Luke stands up and walks off a bit from his mentor.

As Luke sits back down, Yoda, with astonishing concentration, makes the ship rise in the air and places it gently on land. Luke watches in amazement. He walks over to the ship. He touches it. Then walking over to Yoda he says, "I don't—I don't believe it." Without missing a beat, Yoda responds, "That is why you fail."

What an unlikely place to find wisdom. But wisdom nonetheless it is. Yoda knew. And from this parable we can learn so much. More certainly than meets the eye.

Inference

In education, so much energy is spent on the concept of *trying*. The problem with our use of the word "trying" is we infer from it there can be two results, that of success or failure. In that way, if we do something, we either do it successfully and correctly, or we fail at doing it. The latter being thought of as a mistake. The opposite of doing is really *not doing* rather than failing. *Not doing* is simply the fact that we have not done something yet.

We project success or failure on our activities. Thus we are the authors of our fulfillment. Robert Greene Ingersoll stated it so very clearly, "In nature, there are neither rewards nor punishments; there are consequences." Consequences are a result, a fact. Reward or punishment is all in our perception of what we have done. We cannot infer failure as a reaction to "do not." For if so, we imply that result is a mistake, something bad.

What then is a mistake? That word usually conjures up images of bad or incorrect. It is not. It is simply our perception of what we have done. If we, as Yoda put it, "do," then we have done what we have sought to do. If we, again in his words, "do not," we have not failed, we just haven't done it.

Do

Doing something is, in and of itself, succeeding. The final goal may not be reached. The result of our *doing* may not yet be what we want, but the act of doing is positive.

Frustration

With that way of thinking, our students should find much more patience with themselves. If we have students learning appropriate material in small enough steps, they can "do." Problems arise when we ask for what is not within the bounds of our students' readiness, do not systematically teach each step along the way, do not provide enough time for assimilating the material, or work in such enormous steps as to make learning difficult.

Those issues create a sense of frustration for student and teacher. The goal is less often *too difficult* than it is *too big*, too far between steps rather than too many steps. Small steps allow students to regularly feel as though they can "do." If we make each small step along the path a goal able to be accomplished, we provide opportunities for feeling good, rather than creating frustration at how long it may take to get to the goal. Each stride in the process of *getting there* becomes *gotten there*. This goes a long way toward moving any wall of failure out of view, so it's less likely they will bang their heads on it. We decide what the "do" is to be.

Lots of small forward advances, able to be accomplished, create a sense of pride and fulfillment. Learning becomes far more positive and productive if attempts at "doing" something are thought of as steps, practice, attempts at different approaches, the gaining of strength or the figuring out of a process. Frustration is often less about not seeing the goal, and more about not knowing the steps of how to get there.

We must let circumstances dictate our priorities, let priorities determine our actions, and not become overwhelmed by the task before us. We can't try to do *everything* all at once; we just have to do lots of little *somethings* headed toward it. As Oliver Wendell Holmes stated, "Where we stand is not so nearly as important as the direction we are moving."

Believe!

Poor Luke. Caught by his own words: "I don't believe it." Yoda's wisdom helped Luke to understand. Luke didn't believe in his own abilities *or* what was possible. Either can be destructive. To the former I say, if we believe, anything is possible. Or as Wayne Dyer once wrote, "You'll see it when you believe it." And to the latter, Cicero, the great philosopher, held that one of *The Six Mistakes of Man* was "Insisting that a thing is impossible because we cannot accomplish it." When I think something not doable, I always remember the affirmation of Wernher von Braun, considered the father of the United States space program, "I have learned to use the word 'impossible' with the greatest caution."

Unlearn

Yoda spoke of unlearning. It was not that the skill Luke had learned was wrong and needed to be unlearned, but that he had "learned" or convinced himself that either the task was impossible, or that he was incapable of doing it. It was his mindset that needed to be relearned! Yoda perceived it was

Luke's attitude more than his ability that was standing in the way of his achievement. We have to convince our students of their capabilities, and that everything is possible. Difficulty is not impossibility.

Unimaginable

We must encourage our students to realize they have no idea how far they can go. They can dream of the highest ambitions, strive for what is now incomprehensible. Granted, the higher the expectations the farther one can fall, but if each step is secure, anything is achievable. Will there be obstacles? Sure, but in the words of Frank A. Clark, "If you find a path with no obstacles, it probably doesn't lead anywhere." Anything is possible, obstacles and all. But as Yoda confirmed, we are often our own biggest obstacle. Our self-doubt can be staggering.

Though some doubt is part and parcel of being human, as described by Robert Hughes when he wrote, "The greater the artist, the greater the doubt; perfect confidence is granted to the less talented as a consolation prize." But to counter that I ask you to consider the words of the great Vincent van Gogh: "If you hear a voice within you say 'you cannot paint,' then by all means paint, and that voice will be silenced."

Paramount is getting our students to accept the inconceivable, expect the unimaginable, and achieve the impossible. Kevin McHale said it best, "It's not how good you are, it's how good you can become."

"...Find the Journey's End in Every Step..."

Those words of Ralph Waldo Emerson are as marvelous as any I know. We must enjoy each step of the journey as much as the destination. In the process of learning, each tiny stretch should be embraced and savored. Helping students learn is like turning a piece of wood on a lathe. If we jam the sculpting tool into the spinning wood in an effort to make fast progress, we will gouge the wood and probably ruin it. We patiently and methodically need to proceed in small increments.

But far more important is that we enjoy the process of teaching, and they of learning. Is our only satisfaction the finished product or do we take pleasure in the unfolding of it? When eating a luscious steak dinner, is "getting it consumed" the object of our pleasure or is enjoyment found in the savoring of every mouthful? Is emptying the bottle of a rare vintage wine where we find delight or do we relish every sip? In that we really don't know how far our students can go, we must enjoy the path along the way because we will never know when the *final* goal is at hand, or what it will be. In the words of a wonderful Indian proverb, "There is no one day where you can see a green apple turn into sweet fruit."

Turn *Try* Into *Do, Doing, Done*

Imagine sitting somewhere on the mainland shore looking out on the ocean. Just in sight is an island. That island of fulfillment is where we want our students to go. To the

average person, there is no way to get there. No boat. Too
far to swim. Impossible, they would think. That's because
they are not teachers. We chase the dream of accomplishments, joy, realization and exhilaration for our students.
We, as teachers, can see those "invisible" bridges leading to
the island from any number of directions. But as with anything, those who can see, see. While those who cannot, say
there is nothing to see, instead of taking the time to search
for it. Using the wisdom of Yoda, what follows are a few of
those bridges to help our students reach for and touch their
goals.

POSSIBLE

We must believe that anything we know to be worthwhile
and sound is possible. We need to make our students realize
that with commitment, dedication and desire, the highest
goals are within reach. As Helen Keller affirmed, "We can
do anything we want to if we stick to it long enough." Our
imagination is the only limit. William A. Ward once said,
"If you can imagine it, you can achieve it. If you can dream
it, you can become it." Underestimating is not realizing, as
William Longgood wrote, that "Dreams and dedication are
a powerful combination."

WE MUST INSPIRE

There is no doubt that knowledge is power. Equally true is
that you can lead a horse to water, but not get him to drink.
However, if you make that watering hole look like an oasis,
he may be more inclined to take a sip! If we use the power
of our personality to invigorate our students, they will be
inspired to learn. Robert Frost wrote, "What is required is

sight and insight — then you might add one more: excite."
Seeing the work at hand is one thing. Knowing enough to
offer insight into it is better. But being excited about it is
the spark that will ignite the fire of our students' wanting
to learn.

DOING IS SUCCEEDING

Simply doing something toward the goal is an accomplishment. Not doing removes the fear of "failure" but it also
eliminates any chance of moving forward. As John A. Shedd
so masterfully stated, "A ship in harbor is safe — but that is
not what ships are for." We have all heard that wonderful
analogy to various sports: we miss *every* shot we don't take.
When asked by students which of two paths they should
follow, my usual answer is, "Yes." I don't know which will
be best or more beneficial, but I do know that doing something is good. Inaction rarely leads to accomplishments.

WE *ARE* AS WE ARE THOUGHT TO BE

Those words may seem like I'm saying we should walk off
the mainland toward that island armed with only the *hope*
that our *belief* in a bridge will produce one. I'm not; well, not
completely. As much as that would be crazy, I do believe
that *how we act* is often as important as what we do. As
Goethe asserted, "If you treat an individual as he is, he will
stay as he is. But if you treat an individual the way he ought
to be, he will become what he ought to be and could be." In
the words of Mahatma Gandhi, "You must be the change
you wish to see in the world." So, as the old saying prescribes, "Act as if the quality you seek is already within you
and it will be." If we act the way we want to act, we *will* be

acting the way we want to be acting. If we treat students as if they are acting the way we wish them to, often they will.

NO OBSTACLE IS TOO GREAT

An obstacle is an obstacle. However, it is how it is viewed that makes the difference. It can be thought to stop us, thus preventing our ability to move forward in any way. It can be seen as weighing us down or slowing, rather than halting, our progress toward the goal. But it can also be interpreted as an opportunity to use creativity and imagination. I know that sounds like optimism gone amuck, but we all know it's true!

THERE IS NO TIME LIKE NOW

A fantastic African proverb reminds us that "The best time to plant a tree is twenty years ago, the next best time is today." We are dealt a hand of cards; we may wish that it contains four aces, but if it doesn't we need to work with what we are given toward that end. Today is the foundation of the future. "If we don't change the direction we are going," a Chinese proverb suggests, "we are likely to end up where we are heading."

BACKWARDS COMPLETION PRINCIPLE

This simple theory proposes that one way to figure out the steps to a goal is to envision the moment of its completion, and then work backwards to see how you got there. Sometimes thinking this way offers insights for getting to the goal you would not have imagined otherwise. Using your imagination to think through the progression from the goal back to the starting place also offers an opportunity to think about what you could do differently, what should be changed, or what could be made better or easier along that path. Sometimes viewing our situation from another angle, in this case backwards, allows for clearer vision.

Teach Curiosity

Though we have all heard the following quote, it helps us never to lose sight of the mark. "You can teach a lesson for a day, but if you teach curiosity, you teach for a lifetime." Getting our students to wonder, ponder and debate is wonderful. Getting them to want to search for knowledge is even better. Inspiring them to question any thought that they have reached a plateau of learning is even better still.

Let Go of Baggage

Often it is the weight of *believing* we can't do something that must be "unlearned." That baggage we take with us along the path toward our goal is sometimes the most important thing to be changed. If we teach ourselves something is impossible, and continue to reinforce it, it will be. We must learn to ignore that encumbrance, for it can be of no help to anyone. Henry Ford may have said it best when he remarked, "Whether you think you can or think you can't—you are right."

Nonchalance

Sometimes "trying too hard" can be our undoing. If we work toward ability and understanding that is unfettered by worry, concern and angst, we often will be at our best. As Eugen Herrigel stated in *Zen in the Art of Archery*, "The swordmaster is as unself-conscious as the beginner. The nonchalance which he forfeited at the beginning of his instruction he wins back again at the end as an indestructible characteristic." Remember the reckless abandon with which you did just about everything when you were very young? Do you possess that freedom?

As you watch great artists or athletes, are you struck by how easy they make it look? It seems as effortless as breathing. To them it is. They have come full circle. As beginners they undoubtedly endeavored with not a care in the world. As they began to study, more than likely they added worry and concern to their approach. "Trying" does that. It is only when skill allows for confidence that we can return to those carefree ways, now armed with and fueled by true mastery.

Often as we "learn" we become thwarted by worry of correctness and technique. Once we feel we truly know something, we are freed to allow ourselves to use it with ease. We then are no longer bogged down by the shackles of effort but are free to allow the application of the skill to be nonchalant.

When all is said and done, how best can we help our students "do"? Perhaps the following story may help describe our task. Some time ago, a former student came to me, just beginning her career. She feared she wouldn't know what was most important to teach her students. I wrote this in the hope that these words might in some small way help her on her journey. Her concern was admirable; her quest, transcendent.

For the Child Who Believes

For the child who believes
every height can be climbed,
there is no fear of falling.

For the child who believes
every experience is worthwhile,
there is no journey too long.

For the child who believes
every wrong can be righted,
there is no cause thought impossible.

For the child who believes
every goal is achievable,
there is no worry of failing.

For the child who believes
in the value of hard work,
there is no effort unrewarded.

For the child who believes
in the power of a dream,
there is no destiny unreachable.

Yoda knew. And may his words resonate in the hearts and minds of all of us who teach. For in their simplicity there is wisdom. In their phenomenal power there is the promise of every child. ▩

"When You Wish Upon a Star..."

"Optimist: a person with a positive attitude; someone who tends to take a hopeful and positive view of future outcomes; *see also teacher!*" Well, that last bit wasn't actually part of the definition of an optimist, but it should be. Let's face it; one can't dedicate one's life to teaching without being an optimist. We take those who don't know, and believe we can help them to learn. Who but an optimist could do that? It is part of what we are and what we do. It is education.

Now those who know me are reeling as they read this. Why? Because I am a card-carrying pessimist. In fact, I have elevated pessimism to an art form. My wife's favorite line to me is, "That's right, no matter how dark it gets, keep pulling the shades down." At the office, I am known as the department's resident pessimist. Yes, sadly, it's true.

I must share with you that as I am working on this chapter about being an optimist I am laughing out loud. Why? Because I'm writing it while sitting on an airplane at the end of a runway at LaGuardia Airport where I have been parked for over an hour, on my way out of town. This, after having spent the previous seven hours waiting in the terminal. Thinking optimistically is truly the furthest thing from my mind right now. Whether it's steaming about this flight or most anything else in life, I am a pessimist — about everything *except* teaching. I know it sounds odd, but it's the truth. Without a healthy dose of optimism we can't effectively teach. We must believe we can educate and inspire our students and that they can learn and flourish.

Hope

It isn't a case of seeing the glass half empty or half full. We must go even further and see the glass as *twice as big as it needs to be*. Always hopeful, even — or should I say especially — when our students or those around us don't see much reason to be hopeful. As the remarkable Christopher Reeve said, "There's no such thing as false hope — just hope."

Perfection

One must not let *the perfect* become the enemy of *the possible*. That may be one of the most important things we can teach our students. How often does a fear of not doing "it" *perfectly* stop us from trying at all? It's far easier to be a pessimist and say, "I won't be able to do it perfectly, so why try at all," than to try and see if it's possible. Our students need to learn from our example, and support, that perfection is unattainable for most things in life. Our striving for making something possible is virtually the only thing *that is* truly perfect!

Confidence

Our optimism can also help those entrusted to us to believe in themselves. What could be more optimistic? They need to learn that hoping and dreaming yields results when they *believe*. As the old expression goes, "Goals are simply dreams with deadlines." One evening at the dinner table my then-teenaged daughter, Meredith, summed it up better than I ever could, saying, "When you wish upon a star, you are really talking to yourself." To this day, I marvel at the stunning power of those words. Wishes can come true with a heartfelt measure of optimism. But every teacher *knows* that.

"Don't Hide Your Light Under a Bushel"

Teachers are an amazing lot. Our days are filled with so many tasks that we couldn't begin to list them in detail. Even if we could, why bother because no one would believe us. Between the amount of time teaching, planning and sequencing material, writing lesson plans, studying information, corresponding with parents and administrators, not to mention hall duty, designing bulletin boards, phone calls, paperwork, meetings, and the always-on-call "counseling" practice you make available to everyone in your classroom, we have little time for the other 6,371 things we do every day.

We're constantly pulled in so many different directions. We are juggling so many balls in the air at one time, it is often hard to keep track of them, let alone juggle them. Though we often get tired (how's that for an understatement!) and sometimes get anxious (stop laughing and then read: crazed) we get it all done. My concern is all too often the casualty of this intensely demanding occupation is *us*.

Don't get me wrong. I'm not talking about the quality of our teaching or the talent for what we do. I am not speaking of our commitment, dedication or ability. I'm talking about how we are *perceived* by our students. Does our huge workload manifest itself in a way that makes us come across to our students as angry, stressed, impatient, frustrated, short-tempered, unhappy or depressed?

We obviously love teaching and are dedicated to the education of those entrusted to us. We wouldn't still be teaching if we weren't. Quite simply, it's not our knowledge or ability that is diminished by this pace, it's our enthusiasm for what we do and for what our students are doing. We are often so drained by our responsibilities that something must give. We won't shirk any task because we are too dedicated; as a result, sometimes we just can't muster the energy to show our enthusiasm. But we must. At any cost, it must shine through to all.

I hope you have read the heartwarming book *Tuesdays with Morrie* I mentioned in an earlier chapter. It is a life-changing, life-affirming experience. In it Professor Morrie Schwartz offers lessons on "life." Since reading that book, when confronted by a problem, I often wonder what advice Morrie would give me. What would Morrie say about the problem we just described? Some years ago, I was told he particularly liked an old proverb that offers the counsel, "Don't hide your light under a bushel."

But what is our light? Is it our knowledge? I don't think so. I am convinced our light is our enthusiasm. Our knowledge, talent and skill are *in us*, but that "light" of enthusiasm and excitement is necessary for all our students *to see it*! A porch light simply shows you where the door to a home is located so you know where to enter to find the joy of what's inside.

That light of our enthusiasm is what helps generate in our students a feeling of excitement for our subject and for the process of learning it. Our light of enthusiasm sets a positive mood in the classroom. It encourages our students to concentrate with intensity. Clearly, our students look toward us to be a source of knowledge, but, even more, they look toward us to be the source of energy and excitement for the journey to attain that knowledge. From that light they will come to realize how much we love what we teach and how excited we are to share it with them.

We can never underestimate what our enthusiasm does for our students. They may not know what reaching the goal will feel like. They may not understand all they will need to learn to get there. They may not even understand why they are going there at all. But they will sense, from our excitement for what we do, that it is worth the effort.

Will we continue to be stressed? Yes. Will we have those days where our battery is blinking the low-voltage warning light? You bet. Will the level of our enthusiasm and excitement always be vulnerable to the strains of our work? Absolutely. But the next time you walk into a class with the weight of our profession on your shoulders, or feel wiped out from fatigue, or have simply had a rotten day, before you allow anything to take its toll on your enthusiasm, think of Morrie. I guarantee if you have read the book or have seen the movie, you wouldn't — no, you couldn't — ever dream of letting yourself hide your light under a bushel.

Put simply, we must check our problems at the door as we walk into our classes. I know that's easier said than done, but what's at stake is far too important to settle for anything less. A few years ago I was given the following story. In its simplicity is glorious advice.

The Small Tree

The plumber I hired to help me restore an old farmhouse had just finished a rough first day on the job. A flat tire made him lose an hour of work, his electric drill quit and now his ancient one ton truck refused to start. While I drove him home, he sat in stony silence. On arriving, he invited me in to meet his family. As we walked toward the front door, he paused briefly at a small tree, touching the tips of the branches with both hands.

When opening the door he underwent an amazing transformation. His tanned face was wreathed in smiles and he hugged his two small children and gave his wife a kiss. Afterward he walked me to the car. We passed the tree and my curiosity got the better of me. I asked him about what I had seen him do earlier.

"Oh, that's my trouble tree," he replied. "I know I can't help having troubles on the job, but one thing's for sure, those troubles don't belong in the house with my wife and the children. So I just hang them up on the tree every night when I come home and ask God to take care of them. Then in the morning, I pick them up again. Funny thing is," he smiled, "when I come out in the morning to pick 'em up, there aren't nearly as many as I remember hanging up the night before."

Every time I read that story I am reminded of how important it is for my "light" to shine every time I teach. My enthusiasm cannot be diminished by troubles, stress or fatigue. So, following the wisdom of that plumber, I use my office doorknob as my trouble tree. I know it seems ridiculous, but I do. Each time I close the door on my way to teach, I hold that handle for a brief moment and remember what is truly important. Then I am free to be the teacher I want to be. Yes, I am fully aware "reality" will be waiting for me when I pick up that "baggage" as I open my office door upon my return, but for that brief time I am free of anything that could drain my enthusiasm. Is it a bit silly? Yes, it probably is, but I know I am a better teacher because of it. Try it. It certainly is easier than planting a small tree in the hallway outside your classroom!

We know how important our enthusiasm is. It lights a path. And we know that path is too valuable, too precious, too profound, too fragile to risk any single student getting lost or falling without our light. That's just what we teachers do. Morrie knew. Boy, did he know. I wish for our profession, and for all those who are entrusted to it, that his wisdom will never be diminished by his passing. Let us all hope to have a light as brilliant and powerful as his, and allow no bushel ever to cause it harm.

WHY DO WE TEACH?

Have you ever asked yourself that question? More important, have you ever been able to answer it? If you are anything like me, your answer can be short and simple, or lofty and philosophical. It is, however, sometimes difficult to describe to others. When I think about that question, I always remember back to something the composer Vaclav Nelhybel said to me many years ago while we worked together writing his biography. One day I asked him *why* he composed. His answer has stayed with me, echoing in my mind. In the most reverent tone he said, "Composing is the best means for me to manifest my existence as a human being…to communicate with those that I have never met, and those that I will never meet…giving me the satisfaction of knowing that I have spent my life meaningfully."

Isn't that why we teach? You may agree with the first and last part of that quote, but wonder if the middle is relevant to teaching. That is the most important part of all. Think about it: when we teach young people the joys of learning and the important lessons about hard work, teamwork, handling failure and believing in the power of their dreams, we encourage them to teach those lessons to their children, and they to their children. By helping those whom we teach to become caring people, they will pass those qualities along to generations we will never meet. In that way, we will change the lives of human beings farther than we see, and for longer than we can imagine.

We all know there will be frustrations, not the least of which is having students forget what we thought they learned. But those frustrations pale by comparison to the importance of our mission. That's why we teach. Because teaching *is* the best means for us to manifest our existence as human beings, to communicate with those we have never met, and those we will never meet, giving us the satisfaction of knowing we have spent our lives meaningfully. Rich is the man or woman who can look into the eyes of a child and see pride, satisfaction, a tear, a smile. What better way could there be to spend one's life? As Ken Hudgins states, "The meaning of life is to give life meaning." All teachers do just that for themselves, their students and for many whom they will never know.

The answer to why we teach can be found in every educator's heart, but one day I found the answer on the floor. During a lunch break while visiting a high school to present a workshop, I was asked if I wanted a tour of their new building. Though still under construction, it was beautiful. My host and I walked the hallways admiring the quality of the workmanship and design. At one point, we were standing in what was to be the new lobby of the school. Embedded in the floor was a large replica of the school's seal. Looking down on that seal, I saw the words of the school's motto. There I found the answer to why we teach, written to inspire every student ever to enter the building: "Today we follow. Tomorrow we lead." And lead they will. How's that for summing up the influence of *every* teacher?

THE THINGS THAT
MATTER

I have always felt that one of the most important aspects of working with young people is helping them to discover and to express their emotions. Though we all do this in our own way it surely must be one of the great benefits of education. To that end I try my best to show how great art, poetry, literature, music, dance and language make me feel as I teach, hoping my example may help those more reticent students explore their feelings. And it is always a joy to watch their faces as they reveal those emotions.

However, nothing that important comes without risk. The risk we take is that those students who are uncomfortable with those emotions may express their discomfort with nervous giggles. It's human nature: people often laugh when ill at ease. But if we are committed to the goal of helping students to express themselves we must be willing to take that risk. The truth be known, I find that as long as students know our emotions are sincere, the giggles are rare indeed. Though one such time a student really got the better of me.

I was conducting a large honors band of delightful high school students, which could just as easily have been a first-grade lesson on poetry, a sixth-grade art class, or a ninth-grade English class. They were extremely talented and very focused but extraordinarily reserved. I don't just mean polite and quiet, I mean seemingly unmoved by the music they were making; their faces revealing little, their playing much the same. So I worked at getting them to *feel* as much as *think*, to express emotion as much as demonstrate facility. I tried my best to show them what I was feeling with hopes they would do the same through their music. Slowly, almost one by one, they started to blossom. It was wonderful: ninety young people playing from the heart. However, the more emotion I showed, the more one young oboe player made her discomfort apparent with overt giggles. I just couldn't reach her; I was sure she just didn't get it.

This went on, more or less, throughout the first day. By the middle of the second day she wasn't giggling, but seemed unmoved by all around her. I was convinced I had failed to get through to her. Maybe she just wasn't willing to share her feelings. I decided I would have to accept the fact that outward expressions of emotion just weren't part of this young lady's personality.

By the third day, the day of the concert, the students were "playing the spots off the page." They were playing at a level beyond their years. There wasn't a single moment in the entire program I was worried about—except one. It was a very exposed English horn solo at the start of a slow and somber work. The young boy playing the part tried diligently, but it demanded extremely soft and sustained playing, ending with a very long tone on the worst note of the instrument.

Each time we rehearsed the passage it was basically a "coin toss" as to whether that last note, let alone a few of the others, would speak. By concert time I think we all feared the worst for this solo but hoped for the best. Though I was willing to have another instrument play the part as cued by the composer, the young man would have none of it. He was determined to play every note, and I mean every note, of the solo. We all knew the risk that came with that decision but we also knew in our hearts that he had earned the right to try.

Well the evening concert was upon us. The students took their seats on stage, the young man playing the English horn solo seated right next to the seemingly aloof oboist. The concert began. The ensemble played the first five pieces of the performance with exceptional precision and with remarkable expression. I could not have been prouder of them — or so I thought. But now the moment I feared was at hand. It was time for the work we all had a certain amount of trepidation about. Before starting the piece, I gave the young man playing the worrisome English horn solo a smile with the most confident look I could muster, though I must say the look he returned was a bit less comforting. Nonetheless, we started.

The first note of his solo spoke with resolute clarity. The joy we all felt was amazing but we also knew the biggest hurdle was still ahead. And as that last note sounded with the subtlety and dignity of the most seasoned professional musician, we all beamed with delight. He had done it. The entire ensemble, and its conductor, breathed a giant sigh of relief coupled with a surge of intense exhilaration. The powerful emotions we all felt were palpable. As the piece continued I looked him in the eyes, nodded and smiled from ear to ear. He smiled back with a grin that was as full of pride as it was relief.

A few seconds later, I guess just wanting to make sure he hadn't passed out, I glanced back over at him. And just when I thought nothing could make that moment more special, I watched as the oboist I feared I couldn't reach, with a tear running down her cheek, took her hand and patted the knee of that young man with all the sincerity, compassion and sensitivity you could imagine. Like a big sister wanting to show her little brother he had "done good," she looked him in the eyes and spoke from the heart without saying a word. How lucky I was to witness that sight, for it was one of the most touching, extraordinarily emotional displays I have ever seen.

It's amazing how gifts come to us in different packages and how people express emotions in many different ways. Whether from the poignancy of a painting, the proportions of a photograph, the subtlety of a dance, the passion of a poem, the sentiment of a story or the grandeur of an architectural wonder, I guess we just have to do our best to help students express themselves in whatever way they choose, whenever they can, however they are comfortable. We've all been there, wondering whether we got through to a student. During those few days I thought I had lost that young lady; I hadn't. I just didn't know where to look. I thought she "just didn't get it"; she had. She knew what really mattered.

I'm so glad I caught that scene out of the corner of my eye for my life is richer for having done so. The emotional power of what we do, and the capacity of our students to bring it to life, have never ceased to amaze me, and probably never will. ■

"Even a Fool Knows You Can't Touch the Stars..."

What a pessimistic title. But isn't that what we as teachers do? We try to get our students to "touch the stars" every moment of every waking day. So is that quest the ultimate in "tilting at windmills"? Is it foolish even to try? Well, that quote started me thinking, and I realized that being a teacher *is just that*. We help young people reach for the stars. But according to that quote, it's futile. That led me to a very good question: what's at the core of people who would dedicate their lives to something that futile? Otherwise put, what is at the heart of being a teacher? I really wanted to know for two reasons: to help me explain it to others, and more important, to remind myself of the teacher I want to be. Sadly, not the teacher I *am* every day, but the teacher I *want to be* every day.

In addition to being futile, isn't trying to touch the stars risky? You bet. But isn't there some risk in every worthwhile pursuit? Doesn't growth require us to take risks? And isn't that a lesson we want our students to learn? Janet Rand stated it so very eloquently: "The person who risks nothing, does nothing, has nothing, is nothing, and becomes nothing. He may avoid suffering and sorrow, but he simply cannot learn, feel, change, grow or love. Chained by his certitude, he is a slave; he has forfeited his freedom. Only the person who risks is truly free."

But what *is* the risk in trying to touch the stars? Fear we won't be able to reach them? Fear of looking silly for trying so hard? Fear of traveling unfamiliar paths? Fear of stepping into the unknown? Probably a bit of all of those come into play. Maybe it's just a matter of remembering, as Patrick Overton wrote, "When you come to the edge of all the light you have, and must take a step into the darkness of the unknown, believe that one of two things will happen: either there will be something solid for you to stand on, or, you will be taught how to fly." Isn't that a wonderful sentiment? We often don't know when or where growth and learning will come to us. And we all know that some of the greatest accomplishments occur while we are trying to do something very different. So we don't end up touching the stars; settling for touching the moon isn't so bad.

Or is the fear merely a lack of confidence? Are we afraid to try simply because we doubt our ability? Does our image of who and what we are—or, more disconcertingly, who and what we can become—prevent us from even trying to touch those stars? "It's not what you are that holds you back," warns Denis Waitley, "it's what you think you are not." Truer words may not exist.

I guess it doesn't matter whether it's a fear of failure, a fear of stepping outside comfort zones, or a lack of confidence.

A big part of our job is convincing our students to reach, despite the fact that "Even a fool knows you can't touch the stars…." In thinking further, I realize we do that by *whom* we teach, *what* we teach and *how* we teach.

Whom We Teach

Whom *do* we teach? Every student we see. From the cream of the crop — the best and the brightest — to those who struggle at every turn. It doesn't matter, we teach all of them. As Robert D. Ramsey observed, the magic of that is, "You have to stay ahead of the fastest pupil and remain right alongside the slowest pupil at the same time."

We see in them, every one of them, unlimited potential. We look at *every* student like a sculptor looks at a block of marble. We see in them what others, even they, can't see. It's like when the great Michelangelo created his magnificent statue of David, a statue he created from a single piece of marble — a piece of marble other sculptors looked at and refused to work on because it had an enormous flaw running through almost the entire slab. When he was asked how he did it, Michelangelo responded, "I saw the angel in the marble and carved until I set him free. David was always in the marble."

Simply put, we envision what our students can become and then we work to make it happen. We see what's possible, and then *teach* until we set them free to be what they can be. It is then they realize our goal: what once was *never imagined* possible, is *now* possible. It doesn't matter whether our students move in giant steps or baby steps, take to it naturally or with great effort. We take them from where they are — how they are — and gently help them try to touch the stars. Whenever I think of that, I am reminded of the wonderful story that follows. It is as heartening as it is appropriate to the question of *whom* we teach.

The Pot That Was Cracked

An elderly Chinese woman had two large pots. Each hung on the ends of a pole which she carried across her shoulders. One of the pots had a crack in it, and at the end of the long walk from the stream to her house arrived only half full. The other pot, however, was perfect and always delivered its full measure of water.

For a full two years this went on daily, with the woman bringing home only one and a half pots of water. Of course, the perfect pot was proud of its accomplishments. But the poor cracked pot was ashamed of its own imperfection, and miserable that it could only do half of what it had been made to do.

After two years of what it perceived to be bitter failure, it spoke to the woman one day by the stream. 'I am ashamed of myself, because this crack in my side causes water to leak out all the way back to your house.' The old woman smiled, 'Did you notice that there are flowers on your side of the path, but not on the other pot's side? That's because I have always known about your flaw, so I planted flower seeds on your side of the path, and every day while we walk back, you water them. For two years I have been able to pick these beautiful flowers to decorate the table.

So you see, without you being just the way you are, there would not be this beauty to grace the house.'

Each of us has our own unique flaws. But it's the cracks and flaws we each have that make our lives together so very interesting and rewarding. We just have to take every person as they are, and each of us remember to smell the flowers on our side of the path.

What We Teach

What *do* we teach? Yes we teach facts, skills and knowledge, but those are simply vehicles for so much more. We give our students a glimpse of their potential, a window to their soul and a foundation from which to flourish and grow. We teach them how to express themselves, allow them to develop into caring people, and in so doing help mold the future for generations we will never see.

We help young people understand their world, work with others, examine, focus, extrapolate, explain, question and appreciate. That's why trying to enumerate all that we teach is so difficult. But in that frustration I am reminded of the incredible words of Albert Einstein: "Not everything that can be counted counts and not everything that counts can be counted."

How We Teach

The obvious answer is that we use techniques, methods, codified approaches, and the resources of years of training. But that is only the tip of the iceberg. How do we *really* teach? To me, the answer comes from the words of Edith Wharton, who stated, "There are two ways of spreading light: to be the candle or the mirror that reflects it."

We can be the candle, training and teaching our students facts, concepts, knowledge and techniques. But more important, far more important, we can be the mirror, helping them see their accomplishments, the beauty they create and the miracle they are. We want students to appreciate themselves, enjoy hard work, treasure every moment of their lives, learn to give of themselves, learn to invest in themselves and savor the world. We each do that by being a mirror, reflecting back upon our students, simply showing them what had been there all along: themselves.

With all that said, I have come to know that "what's at the heart of being a teacher" *is* the essence of the simple quote I started this chapter with: "Even a fool knows you can't touch the stars...." However, I guess I should tell you *the rest* of the quote. It comes to us from Judge Harry T. Stone, the indomitable character played by Harry Anderson on the television show "Night Court," in which the venerable jurist so exquisitely stated, "Even a fool knows you can't touch the stars, but it doesn't stop a wise man from trying." But you already knew that, because that's what every teacher knows, believes and lives. Whether our students ever get close to a star or not, they will be all the better for having tried. ▨

THE SPIRIT OF
THE GIFT

In his wonderful book, *All I Really Need to Know I Learned in Kindergarten*, Robert Fulghum tells the story of V. P. Menon, a man of humble beginnings who rose to become a significant political figure during India's struggle for independence from Britain. Menon, the eldest of twelve children, quit school at thirteen to work as a laborer before taking a job as a government clerk. Rising to the highest ranks, he was eventually praised by both Nehru and Lord Mountbatten for his important role in helping to bring freedom to his homeland. He was also known for his charity, explained by Fulghum with the following story.

"When Menon arrived in Delhi to seek a job in government, all his possessions, including his money and I.D., were stolen at the railroad station." "In desperation he turned to an elderly Sikh, explaining his troubles, and asking for a temporary loan of fifteen rupees to tide him over until he could get a job. The Sikh gave him the money. When Menon asked for his address so that he could repay the man, the Sikh said that Menon owed the debt to any stranger who came to him in need, as long as he lived. The help came from a stranger and was to be repaid to a stranger.

"This story was told to me by a man whose name I do not know. He was standing beside me in the Bombay airport at the left-baggage counter. I had come to reclaim my bags and had no Indian currency left. The agent would not take a traveler's check, and I was uncertain about getting my luggage and making my plane. The man paid my claim-check fee — about eighty cents — and told me the story as a way of refusing my attempts to figure out how to repay him. His father had been Menon's assistant and had learned Menon's charitable ways and passed them on to his son."

Fulghum goes on to write, "The gift was not large as money goes, and my need was not great, but the spirit of the gift is beyond price and leaves me blessed and in debt."

In so many ways I think this story describes education. Every moment we teach aren't we continuing a similar cycle? Our teachers helped us learn, not so we may repay that knowledge back to them, but so we can pass it on to others, who in turn may pass it on to still others.

As well, every time we empower children to stand on their own, dream of more than they thought possible, cherish their world or delight in their potential, aren't we in fact helping them to share *those* very gifts with others, who will continue to share them? Those gifts may indeed not be "large as money goes," but they are truly priceless and timeless.

As that wise old Sikh passed his gift to Menon, who passed it on to his assistant, who passed it on to his son, who passed it on to Robert Fulghum, who passed it on to me, who passed it on to you so that you can pass it on to others, so go the subject lessons, and more important, the life lessons our students learn from us.

Will any one deed change the world? Can any small event change a life? Who knows. But surely all we do will travel far beyond the walls of our schools through the minds, hearts and souls of our students. It is a profound responsibility but also an amazing opportunity. We must cherish that notion, guard it, honor it and savor it. For long after we are gone the essence of who we were and what we did, the spirit of those gifts, will forever be carried on by those whom we have taught.

I guess it all boils down to the simple power of the words of Bruce Barton: "Sometimes when I consider what tremendous consequences come from little things…I am tempted to think…there are no little things."

BREAK A LEG

Have you ever thought about that phrase? I mean ever *really* thought about it. We use it all the time, bantering it around to our colleagues and students as a frothy way of wishing them luck. You've probably had it said to you as often as you've said it to others as a sarcastic quip of humorous irony and incongruous wit. However to me those words are anything but silly, anything but amusing. In fact the power of that phrase grounds me with its importance, excites me with its promise and reminds me of the solemn responsibility of our work every time I hear it.

Though there are many explanations for how that odd trio of words can be explained and has found its way into common usage, the one I choose to believe comes from the days of Victorian theater. A time that "proper" was the order of the day and formality was as important as correctness. Legend has it that as actors or actresses took the stage, those three words would be said to them by their fellow performers to encourage them to have a fabulous performance. Not as a cute, superstitious, tongue-in-cheek "slap on the back," but as an ardently serious hope.

For you see, back then, if an actor's performance was very good and met with the audience's approval he was permitted to come to the edge of the stage and bow with a sincere nodding of the head as the rest of his body stayed straight and tall. If the performance was so appreciated as to receive great applause he was allowed to bow by bending forward from the waist. But if the actor's work was so special, so fantastic, so extraordinary as to have the audience respond with a rousing ovation, then the actor could come to the edge of that stage and bow by putting one foot out in front of him as he almost bent down on one knee, so as to truly *break a leg*.

To me this simple phrase is a reminder of how important we are in the lives of our students, how we must cherish every opportunity to nurture them, how great a responsibility education is and how each moment of our teaching must be the best we can muster. It reminds me that the promise we make as teachers is humbling, the promise each new day holds is limitless and the promise each student possesses is infinite. It helps me remember the joys of teaching, those gifts which are as intangible as they are amazing. For whatever the name we call teacher, and there are many, the rewards may be as subtle as an unspoken word, as simple as a tentative smile or as poignant as a tender tear.

The phrase brings focus to the goal of our own planned obsolescence, teaching students as much about *how* to learn and *why* the joy of learning is as exciting as the subject matter itself. It reassures me that the greatest gift we can give our students is the knowledge they can move beyond our time with them, confident they no longer need us. For we surely know that the real gifts we receive are ultimately those we give. As Pericles so succinctly put it, "What you leave behind is not what is engraved in stone monuments, but what is woven into the lives of others." Or in the words of St. Francis: "Remember that when you leave this earth, you can take nothing you have received…but only what you have given…."

As teachers we can do no better than to remember, "We never know how far-reaching something we may think, say, or do today will affect the life of a child tomorrow." Those *tomorrows* that we plant today for every child, confident in the wisdom of Robert Lewis Stevenson who cautioned, "Don't judge each day by the harvest you reap, but by the seeds you plant." Those *seeds* that will always be a part of each student we teach, or as Rodger Austin so perfectly stated, "Sometimes people, who come into your life, make changes in you…because you always take a little part of them with you into the future. We are all made up of little bits and pieces of those whose lives touch ours."

Reflect for a moment on those amazing teachers in your life and the little bits and pieces of them you took with you, that you keep with you, that you cherish, that help make you who you are today. Those are the little bits and pieces which every one of your students will take with them: a spoken word or simple deed, an igniting thought or knowing smile.

No words express this better than those which follow. They have been attributed to many and though we may never truly come to know their author, the power of the sentiment crystallizes who we are and what we do as teachers: "Watch your thoughts, for they become words. Watch your words, for they become actions. Watch your actions, for they become habits. Watch your habits, for they become character. Watch your character, for it becomes your destiny." Far more important, as teachers our thoughts, words, actions and habits will help shape the character and destiny of each of our students. That, my friends, is *our* destiny, is *our* legacy, is what John Allston meant when he counseled, "The only thing you take with you when you're gone is what you leave behind."

We all know teachers rarely leave behind massive fortunes that can be counted or colossal monuments that can be filmed. But in so many ways teachers are quiet heroes in the lives of their students. Heroes that make a difference in ways that are intangible, invisible and unknowable but are nonetheless as rich as any fortune, as grand as any monument. I guess our destiny as teachers can best be explained in the words of the popular video game *Halo* 3 which affirms, "A hero need not speak. When he is gone, the world will speak for him." As teachers much of our world is our students and they indeed will speak for us, now and long after we are gone.

So with all this and much more at stake, it is clear our work is much more than a career, it's a calling. A calling we were drawn to by the promise of the joy it holds for us, our students and all of humanity. Who knows whether we chose this calling or it chose us, but either way, let us hope that each of us may work to teach so well as to earn the title of teacher, to finish each of our days, each of our years and ultimately each of our careers confident we deserve to *break a leg*. ◾

"I ALWAYS THOUGHT
I HAD TOMORROW"

"Dear Peter, I'm writing to you because I thought you could help. But I know you can't. No one can." So the letter began from a music teacher friend of mine. "Yesterday was just a normal day around here. I started with a few rehearsals, then a couple of lessons, my normal lunch and hall duty, ending with a rehearsal last period. It wasn't the best day of my teaching career, but it wasn't the worst day either. It was just a normal average day. After school, I taught a couple of make-up lessons, did a little paperwork, made a few phone calls and headed off for home. It was just normal. It was just average.

"Then I heard the news. On her way home from school, a student, one of my students, was in a car accident. She died at the scene. Word went around our small town like wildfire. It hit me like a ton of bricks. This wasn't some nameless, faceless person I saw on the front page of a newspaper; it was one of my students. She wasn't the best alto sax player I ever had but she was one of mine.

"I keep trying to remember back to that last period rehearsal we had together, wondering if I made it matter. I just don't know. I know I didn't holler at her, or say anything mean to her. But I don't remember much of anything else either, because it was just a normal average day.

"Now, everything I thought I knew is different. My life changed yesterday. Nothing seems the same. Nothing will be normal again. I wish I had told her how proud I was of her, that she was doing better and that I appreciated her effort. I wish I had made her smile or given her that pat on the back. But I didn't, and now I can't.

"I know there is nothing I can do now, and there is nothing you can say, but I just needed to share this with someone. I wish I had done any of those things. When I think about it, I guess I didn't because I always thought I had tomorrow. But for her, I never had tomorrow."

There have been very few times in my life that I have been rendered speechless. Reading that letter was one of them. I didn't know what to say. I didn't know what to do. I sat and looked at a blank computer screen with tears streaming down my face, not having any idea what to write. He was correct: there was nothing I could say. No words could console him, no words could help him, no words could make it better.

As I sat there helpless, thoughts of my own students filled my head. How often they must leave my classes not knowing how much they matter. How often I assume that with enough tomorrows I'll get to making them all feel special. Sadly there aren't always those tomorrows.

Over the weeks that followed that day, I thought—ever more fervently—about the time I had with my students and how very precious it was. I became more conscious of every moment. While teaching, I often found myself looking at a student, thinking, "What if these are the last words we share?" What would I say? What would I find myself someday wishing I would have said? Though I had never thought about it before, I guess I too always thought I had tomorrow. I always thought I had more time. But as Anna Nalick reminds us, "Life's like an hourglass glued to the table." And not only can't we stop those sands of time, or turn that hourglass over, we don't even know how long that hourglass lasts.

Time: that most precious of commodities. The time we have our students in our classes. The time we have our students in our sphere of influence. The time we have to do meaningful things for our students. The time we have to share the joy of learning with them. The time we have to make it matter, to make no day in life a "normal average" day. The time we have to teach our students to value, savor and cherish every passing moment.

My friend was right in so many ways. I couldn't help him. But *he* helped *me*. This tragedy reminded me that no day can be average or normal. Each must be special and treasured, *just like our students*.

I used to believe I had plenty of tomorrows with my students. Since that day, my greatest fear as a teacher is that I won't. I find myself asking whether I would say, do or be anything different if I knew today would be the last time I would see one of my students ever again.

It is said that time is our worst enemy. That may be true, but regret can't be far behind, and for a teacher what greater regret could there be than to be faced with the realization that there will be no more tomorrows for a child?

So now when I look into the eyes of my students I'm

much more careful, much more worried. But I also find more joy, enjoy more smiles and delight more fully in the time I share with them, trying all the while to count that time by the moments that matter rather than the minutes that simply pass. Heaven knows I pray the day will never come when I would have to say the last sentence of his letter—"But for her, I never had tomorrow"—but if I ever do, I hope I can find some comfort in the memories of the precious time we did get to share on this earth together.

I guess life really is that hourglass glued to a table. For tomorrow is a promise given to no one. No one. ▨

"PERCHÉ?"

Funny thing about wisdom, you never know where you'll find it. Sometimes it's found in the pages of a book. Sometimes it's found in the words of a scholar. Sometimes it comes from great teachers. Sometimes it comes from great philosophers. But sometimes it is in the face of a three-year-old child. And how gloriously profound that can be. One such time I will never forget.

I left my hotel room early one morning, stopped by a corner café for a cup of espresso or three, then set out walking around town. As I strolled through this beautiful city I saw gorgeous architecture, stunning facades and breathtaking views interrupted only briefly by the occasional passing fireboat, ambulance boat, police boat, mail boat and *UPS* delivery boat. It was after a few of those I said to myself, "Peter, you're not in Kansas anymore." I wasn't; it was Venice, Italy.

Venice, one of the most amazing places on earth, with its winding maze of canals, is a marvel of ingenuity and resourcefulness. In that my hotel was on one side of town, I decided to spend the day walking across the city seeing as much as I could, meandering from site to site. By late afternoon, there I was on the other side of this celebrated city, standing in the Piazza San Marco staring in awe at the power and grace of the majestic Basilica di San Marco. By day's end, I was exhilarated and invigorated. I was also exhausted.

At that point I decided not to walk back to my hotel, but rather to jump on a water bus. Just like any bus running through any city, it's just that this flotilla of floating public transportation stops at various places as it circumnavigates the Grand Canal. So I wandered over to the stop conveniently located right at the Piazza, checked my map and figured out that I needed the number 82 water bus bound for San Marcuola, the closest stop to my hotel. After only a few moments one pulled up to the dock-stop and I hopped on.

I took my seat on a bench at the front of the boat, right along the railing, in the open air where I planned on taking in as much of the view as possible. Off we went, floating along this beautiful waterway moving from stop to stop. I was captivated by each building, each picturesque scene and the gentle wake of each passing boat. I was truly mesmerized. Then in the distance I saw my stop. San Marcuola now in sight, I moved to the disembarking area of the boat. There I stood and watched as we floated right *past* my stop. Puzzled, I re-checked my map. Sure enough, I *was* right, I *did* need the number 82 boat. Unfortunately, I soon realized, I must not be on one. So I stuck my head over the side and sure enough, there was the placard clearly stating this was a number 4 water bus.

After another check of my map, it seemed the best solution was to take a seat and enjoy the ride all the way around the *entire* city. So I did. I made my way back to my bench seat and sat down for the ride. Though this time, right along the rail next to me sat a beautiful little girl with eyes the size of the sun, though twice as brilliant. On either side of her were her grandfather and grandmother, each with a face wreathed with expressions of love and warmth.

As we traveled along the canal I couldn't help but watch this trio as much as the view around me. At one point I heard the grandfather speak to the little girl as he pointed out something in the water. But since my Italian is even worse than my water-bus choosing, I couldn't understand a single word. Then the little girl looked at him and said, "Perché?" And even though I can't tell a 4 from an 82, I did know her response was a simple "why?"

To that her grandfather rattled off a lengthy answer, only to be followed with another "perché." Unwavering, he eloquently came back with a lengthy explanation which again was followed by another "perché" from this delightful child. This went on for quite some time, the grandfather showing the patience of a saint, the child showing the curiosity of an inventor. I was fascinated by each passing answer and each questioning "why." Over and over, back and forth they went. She wanted to know why and no answer seemed to suffice. I don't know how many times I heard her mantra of "perché," but it went on for some time as we shared this ride around the city of Venice.

After quite a long while, the little girl and her slightly worn-out grandparents came to their stop. As they moved toward the exit, the grandfather nodded to me and waved. "Your granddaughter is charming and delightful," I said to the kindly old man as he smiled with pride. I knew I would never see them again, but I was so glad I took the wrong water bus and providence allowed me to spend some time with them.

Even though I could understand only one word of the lengthy conversation, it reminded me of one of the only things that really matters in teaching: getting a child to ask "why." Not just ask it, but dwell on it, ponder it, stew over it, insist upon it, dream about it and savor it. One little word that can lead a child to discover anything, learn anything and become anything. One word — one simple word — that can change a child's life. I dare say that little or nothing we teach may be as important as never letting a child lose that curiosity, that desire to ask "why." For doesn't everything else flow from that?

Now, I have three children. I have obviously heard my share of "why." So what made that event, that day, on that water bus crystallize into such a powerful experience? What brought it so vividly to mind? I don't know. Maybe it was the magnificence of the surroundings, maybe it was the fact that I understood nothing but that one word, maybe it was because the faces of those people were so captivating, maybe it was because that precious three-year-old child had such powerful intensity, but maybe it was the fact that I only knew the question, not the answer.

I will never forget that city. I will never forget that day. I will never forget that child. But most important, I hope to never forget the power of helping young people cherish the joy of asking "why." If we can simply get students to ask, with just that one word, the mind wanders, the senses percolate, the memory searches and the heart yearns. In short, they will learn to spend their lives finding the answers, because they will have all the right questions.

I know I will never see that charming little girl again but I have no worries about her. I have no doubt she will become nothing less than what she sets her mind to become. Because she surely knows how to look at her world, find the eyes of a loving grandfather and simply ask — no, demand — to know "why."

THE LIST

Have I mentioned how much I appreciate your sharing time with me? And I hope our paths cross soon. It will be wonderful to see you *again*. That's right, "again." You may not remember, but we went to school together. You remember me, don't you? Surely you do! We were in the same class back in school. Remember? I sat in the back row, so you might not remember *me*, but how could anyone forget that amazing person who taught us? That special, unforgettable teacher who made all the difference in the world. Of course you remember who I mean! Can't you just picture her face?

I remember how much she loved what she taught. How much she cared about us. How much our success mattered. More significant, how much we mattered as people. She never crossed the line of demanding too much, but never let us settle for too little. She was the very embodiment of kindness, support, dedication, perseverance, humility, concern, pride, warmth, zeal and passion. She gave freely of her wisdom, heart and soul. No matter how angry she may have ever been with us as students, she was never angry with us as human beings. She cared as much about what she taught as she did about her students. She was as concerned about our growth as students as she was with our growth as people. She was always there with that friendly smile, that knowing grin, and that raised-eyebrow look of worry. She always knew when we goofed, but never made us feel bad. She reveled in our every success. We could go to her with any problem. We could always trust her advice. We could always look to her as a model teacher and person. Can't you remember thinking you wanted to be just like her? I know I did. Wow, I miss her so much.

I hope by now you are saying to yourself: "Maybe he *was* there. Did he have *my* teacher too?" Well, I know her because I had the "same teacher." Mine just happened to be in a small town in Pennsylvania! Indeed, I would venture to say that we all had *that* special teacher, somewhere, at some time. And if we were very, very lucky, we had several of them.

Can't you just picture that teacher? I bet you often find yourself saying: "What would he have done in this situation?" or "How did she do that?" But have you ever stopped to think about what attributes made that person so special? What made him or her different from most every other teacher you had?

A few years ago at the dinner table with my family, we had a discussion about teachers. At the ripe old ages of fourteen, twelve and eight, my children thought they had the perspective to compare all of their previous teachers. The conversation then turned to the teachers my wife and I had at their ages. It got me thinking. Starting with kindergarten and moving forward, I tried to remember each of my teachers, in every subject. I found it interesting that for some of them I could remember their maiden *and* their married names, but for others I couldn't remember anything. Why? Why do I remember Miss Clark (who became Mrs. Paul midyear) from kindergarten, but can't remember any of my high school English teachers? I always thought fondly of my favorite teachers, but I never sat down to wonder why. What made them amazing, and impossible to forget?

Though this may seem like a stroll down "memory lane," I believe it can be far more than simply reminiscing. It is teacher-training at its best. If we take stock of the qualities of those whom we found to be remarkable teachers, and look for commonalities, we can make certain to embody those very qualities. If we take the best attributes from our very best teachers, we will ensure our success, and more important, the success of our students. How did that terrific math teacher handle discipline problems? How did that wise French teacher balance expectations with reality so well? What was it about that art teacher's pacing that made it amazing? What trick did that science teacher use to get us to remember things? What was it about the way that physical education teacher gave directions that made it so easy to understand everything?

Remember those wonderful words of George Santayana, "Those who cannot remember the past are condemned to repeat it." I believe it is equally true that those who remember the best of the past *can* repeat it. We must learn from others' mistakes and failings, just as we learn from our own mistakes and failings. However, we must take the time to remember the wonder of our past teachers' excellence and repeat that, just as we repeat our own excellent moments as teachers. We can never forget that those faces staring back at us *now* will someday sit at the kitchen table with their children and recall all of *their* amazing teachers. Every day, we must do our best to make certain we are on *their lists*.

As to my list, Mr. Peiffer, my high school band director, would certainly be near the top. I am sure you had a Mr. Peiffer. I would watch him teach and think: "That is *what* I want to be." Little did I know what I really meant was, "That is *who* I want to be." I didn't know if he was the finest band director on the planet or the best teacher who ever held a baton. It certainly wasn't that we always saw eye to eye. But he was incredible in so many ways. He was always the teacher, always prepared and eager, always a gentleman, always the mentor, always the cheerleader, always the role model. He never let us give up on ourselves. He never let us settle for less than our best. He always praised the little steps along the way. He was always dedicated, fair, honest and encouraging. He truly loved what he taught and shared that love with all those whom he taught. He was always ready to give extra time or explain the next step along the way. He meant the world to me.

I remember one day in particular. Back in high school, two of us were chosen to attend a festival on the other side of the state. Mr. Peiffer drove us there. We left very early in the morning and drove for what seemed like an eternity. On our arrival, we had dinner at a restaurant near the host school. After dinner we decided to take a walk around the town to stretch our legs after that interminably long car ride. We walked and talked for a good couple of hours. The conversation was filled with dreams, hopes, aspirations and worries. Mr. Peiffer spoke of how wonderful life and teaching were and how bright and successful he was sure our lives would be. He gave me confidence and counsel. As

long as I may live, I will never forget that walk or that conversation. I have replayed it time and time again. That was
Mr. Peiffer. What a gem of a person. I always respected and
cherished him, even when I was mad at him, and I hope he
sensed how much I appreciated him. I hope I thanked him
enough. But I know in my heart, I never really did.

After graduating from high school and moving on to
college, I spent many moments thinking of Mr. Peiffer, with
most of that time spent realizing how much I owed to him
and how I really needed to sit down and thank him. As that
feeling grew, I planned a trip home with the intent of taking
Mr. Peiffer out to lunch and finally getting that chance to
truly express my appreciation for all he had given me. I was
very excited. I drove home, pulled into the driveway of my
parent's house, walked up to the front door where I was met
with a big kiss and hug from my mom. But I could tell something was wrong. She handed me a note, and told me that
she had received a phone call to let us know that Mr. Peiffer
had died suddenly. I was devastated. I was so very saddened
at the thought of his passing, but I was more upset at the
thought that he had died without my ever getting the chance
to say "thank you." That opportunity was now gone forever.
Even all these years later, I realize Mr. Peiffer—always the
teacher—though no longer with us, had taught me a valuable lesson: Never put off thanking someone when you have
the chance, for that chance may disappear forever.

I tell that story to every group of students I teach. I ask
all of them to go home and thank *their* teachers. I tell them
that whether it is with a note or a pat on the back, they
need to thank the people who helped make them *who* and
what they are today. I tell them *not* to make the same mistake

I made. Sadly, though, many young people are shy or have trouble expressing themselves in words. So as I come to a close, I would like to take this opportunity to express to you what each and every one of your students wants to say, but like me, probably never took the time to say:

Thank you for being you.
Thank you for being there when I needed someone to talk with about a problem.
Thank you for making me strive to be a better person as well as a better student.
Thank you for showing me how to be dedicated.
Thank you for allowing me to sense wonder, emotion, awe and joy.
Thank you for caring.
Thank you for always giving of yourself.
Thank you for helping me learn to cry.
Thank you for allowing me to grow.
Thank you for showing me what it meant to be a teacher.
Thank you for being dedicated.
Thank you for being honorable.
Thank you for being enthusiastic.
Thank you for all the extra time you gave me.
Thank you for showing me the joys of learning and of life.
Thank you for helping me at every juncture.
Thank you for your wisdom, poise, dignity and intensity.
Thank you for challenging me.
Thank you for never giving up on me even when I gave you reason to.
Thank you for never letting me be less than what I could be.

Thank you for seeing the vision of my successes in the
future, rather than my failures of the past.
Thank you for helping me to become what I am and will be.
Thank you for giving me a sense of pride and worth.
Thank you for showing me the beauty of truth.
Thank you for being you, my teacher.

Goodbye, Mr. Peiffer. I miss you. I hope you know what
you meant to me. But I know the best way to honor you is
to become the best teacher I can be. I only hope someday
to mean as much to one person as you did to me.

"If You Don't Know, I Can't Tell You!"

That's not a very reassuring title for the person about to embark on reading this chapter. You're probably wondering why there are any words on this page at all. It makes me think of one of those speeches given at a banquet. You know, where after eating dinner, the guest speaker is brought to the dais and asked to share everything he knows with all those who are gathered. Now picture if on that banquet program you were to see the words used for this chapter title. You would probably expect the speaker to stand at the lectern, graciously receive the applause, and then begin his speech by firmly saying, "Thank you very much. I can't tell you anything, so I'm going to sit down now," as he walks back to his place at the head table. If you've been to as many banquets as I have, you would undoubtedly agree that would be followed by raucous applause as all in attendance looked around in shock saying, "Now that is how all banquet speeches should be." My experience with dinner speeches all too often has the speaker rant on for thirty minutes or so. Then, as he comes up for air, he utters those words that can make a grown man or woman cry: "Now for the *second* half of my speech...." Those scenes aside, it does seem a bit odd that a chapter with the above title would be longer than one sentence. I can imagine you're thinking: "If he can't tell me something, why is he going on for pages?" Let me try to explain.

The past few years have brought a flurry of interest in and discussion about learning standards, advocacy and justifying the place of every subject in modern education. Those topics are indeed pressing and of great significance. Though they have always been of concern, they seem to have risen to new heights of timeliness and importance. Just like many teachers, I have spent the better part of my career defending my subject as an integral part of a person's education. Over the years of preaching that, we have all gathered vast bits of ammunition about why what we teach should hold its rightful place in the curriculum.

Statements about how we do more than help students raise their SAT scores, we help them develop eye-hand coordination, self-esteem, self-expression, creativity, imagination and self-discipline. We help them learn fractions, but more important, solve problems. We help them learn about historical events and cultures as well as to deal with their emotions. The list goes on and on. But with all we know about what education *does* do, all the testaments from people about how important it has been in their lives, and with all the joy teaching and learning has brought the world, our defense of *any* subject, let alone education itself, should be so unnecessary. Why *do* we have to justify what we do? It seems so obvious to *me*. It seems so simple. I then remembered the words of H. L. Mencken when he stated,

"For every complex problem, there is a solution that is simple, neat, and wrong."

So why do we have to defend any aspect of education? Why do we ever need to defend any subject's place in the curriculum? Why should any discipline be at risk for cuts in staffing, scheduling or budget? Like you, I have always considered learning to be the most important part of my life. *We* could not imagine *our* world without it. So I wanted to know why. Why should any of us have to defend what we do?

I decided I would listen to some of the common arguments leveled against us. I started with that question we have all heard about vocation versus avocation, those pearls of wisdom about how few of our students will become full-time professional musicians, scientist, mathematicians, athletes or linguists, thus making a vocation of their study. Without question that is true. Obviously that argument is ridiculous. We agree that all of what a young person learns goes to making him or her well rounded, learned and experienced. As James Truslow Adams stated, "There are obviously two educations. One should teach us how to make a living and the other how to live."

All too often the second argument we hear is how expensive education is. That is true. When you look at the cost of microscopes, computers, uniforms or books, we are expensive. But when we compare what is spent on education to other fiscal responsibilities of the private and public sectors—let alone the cost to humanity of *not* investing in education—it is a bargain.

After thinking about those arguments, I still had no more of an answer than when I started. So I decided I would study great thinkers. They would undoubtedly have the answers I sought. I read the works of Plato, Socrates and Aristotle. I went back and studied the quadrivium and trivium. Those tenets, still remarkable today, firmly stated what was essential in a person's education. After thinking about what those brilliant individuals espoused, I was more puzzled than ever as to how anyone could still question the value of education or any subject therein. The answer seemed even more elusive.

I decided my next step should be to study great educators. I read the thoughts of John Amos Comenius, the father of modern education and his work represented in *The Great Didactic*. That extraordinary gentleman gave us so much in the way of philosophies and principles of education. I was reminded of the impact he had on education. The true value of education was so clear to me. Why wasn't it that clear to everyone who questioned any aspect of what we do? How could we defend every subject in a way all would understand?

Now with an even greater sense of debilitating frustration, I realized I still had no answer as to why it was so clear to me and seemingly so unclear to many who questioned the importance of education. We obviously must not be explaining it very well. I needed someone wiser than Socrates. Someone more enlightened than Plato. Someone more insightful than Aristotle. Someone more learned than Comenius. Then it hit me: I remembered back to my first teaching experience. Working with an extremely experienced and wonderful gentleman, I was teaching seventh-grade instrumental music. Before the bell rang on my first day, we sat in our office drinking coffee. I was so excited.

Do you remember how excited you were on that first day? I was almost trembling in anticipation. I was about to work with young people. My dream of sharing my love of learning with children was about to be realized. I could hardly contain myself. As we sat there chatting, I heard the sound of a trumpet coming from the band room. Like a Pavlovian dog hearing a bell ring, my adrenaline started to flow! It was clear to me that this young person had come in before school started in order to practice. Immediately, I asked if I should go in and work with him. I was told very calmly that it probably wasn't a good idea. Truly puzzled, but not wanting to rock the boat on my first morning, I sat and drank my coffee while that experienced teacher worked with the student.

The next morning, the scene was replayed. Again, I was told it probably wasn't a good idea for me to go into the band room and work with that young person. By the third morning, I couldn't stand it anymore. I wandered into the band room while my colleague was checking his mail in the main office. There I met a seventh-grade boy by the name of Billy. I asked Billy if he wanted a lesson. He and I spent about twenty minutes that morning working on his trumpet playing. He was a delightful young man. He was very attentive and seemed mature beyond his years. But after a few minutes of working with Billy I noticed that the way in which he lifted the trumpet up before he played appeared to be awkward. It seemed to be with more effort than it should have been. Just before the first bell rang we ended our session and I sent him on his way.

A few days later, as I sat drinking my coffee before school, I again heard the sound of a trumpet. I walked into the band room, and there was Billy. From then on, we worked together most every morning. Over time I realized his odd manner of lifting the trumpet was becoming more labored. With each passing day the movement seemed more filled with effort and discomfort. Eventually it became clear to me that Billy was starting to feel pain each time he lifted his horn. Speaking with other teachers, I was told what I was seeing was a manifestation of the fact that Billy had muscular dystrophy. It seemed his muscles grew tired each time he brought the instrument to his lips. I also came to find out that was why I was advised against working so closely with Billy. No one knew how long he would be with us. As the weeks passed, the energy expended by Billy to play the trumpet was exhausting. It had far less to do with producing a sound than it did with simply holding the instrument up.

My feelings of helplessness grew with Billy's feelings of frustration and fatigue. But he never gave up. It seemed that no frustration would stop him. As months passed it got to the point where Billy would start with the trumpet on his lap, clutching it with both hands. He would then gather up all the power and strength he possessed, and with one burst he would thrust the trumpet up so that the bell, the flared end, was pointing straight into the air. Then as if cushioned with an open parachute, the trumpet started to come down to its normal placement in a slow descent while at the same time Billy set his lips upon the mouthpiece. He would then have a window of opportunity during which he could play his trumpet: from where the bell was just above the horizon until it fell to his lap. The frustration grew to be palpable. I didn't know how to help him.

The first morning of school after the December vacation, I again heard Billy playing his trumpet in the band room. I walked into the room and there he was seated behind some contraption. Watching Billy play over the vacation, his grandfather realized he knew how to help. He took a Christmas tree stand; you know that metal bowl with feet and screws to hold an evergreen in place. He then bent a coat hanger and fashioned a large "V" to act as a holster for the bell of the trumpet. That was attached to the top of a length of two-by-four lumber. The wood was inserted into the stand like the base of a tree. With a few adjustments for height, Billy was ready to go. He would sit behind that gizmo, gather his strength for one good burst of energy, lift the bell in the air, and have it land in the coat-hanger holster. It was inspired. His grandfather saw a problem and found the solution. Now the bottom of that bell did get a bit banged up, but Billy was playing his trumpet with renewed zeal!

It worked so well. But even that couldn't stop the muscles from growing weaker. As time passed, it grew harder and harder for Billy to play his trumpet. It seemed so painful. During one such time in a lesson I asked Billy if he wanted to keep going. He nodded yes. At that moment, I finally gathered the courage to ask him the question that had been on my mind for months. I looked him in the eye and said, "Billy, I have to ask you a question." He said, "What?" I replied, "Why do you do it?" Quite puzzled he said, "Do what?" Gathering my composure I asked, "Why do you still want to play the trumpet so much even though it's causing you such pain?" He turned his head toward me, looked up at me, stared me right in the eyes and said,

"Mr. Boonshaft, if you don't know, I can't tell you!" I stood there dumbfounded. I kept replaying those words over in my head. It was utterly amazing. The power of that simple statement has never left my mind or my heart. He knew. I realized then what that little seventh grader knew all along. He knew words were useless. He was as wise as he was courageous and sincere. Billy expressed in words the inexpressible. He saw the invisible. He heard the inaudible. He knew what words could not express. That little twelve-year-old boy understood.

Remembering what Billy had taught me, I realized that the real reason I couldn't answer my *original* question was that I couldn't put the answer into words that everyone could understand. The problem to me was like trying to describe the *Mona Lisa* in five easy words or less. It was like trying to describe the taste of a wonderful vintage port, the impact of a sunset, or the birth of a child. No wonder those great people in history could never really describe why any part of education was so important. They could only describe the impact it had on them and others. We are trying to use words to describe the indescribable.

I saw a commercial on television once. It was aired only months after the devastating attacks of 11 September 2001 on the United States of America. The commercial showed a team of those spectacular Clydesdale horses walking toward the City of New York from a great distance across a snow-covered field. As the Statue of Liberty and New York City skyline came into sight, the horses stopped, looked at what was before them, and were seen to bow. No words were spoken; no text was written. Only a group of horses bowing in reverence. I sat watching with tears in my eyes.

It was a powerful sight. But as powerful as it was, what took it to the core of every person who watched was what they could bring to it: appreciating events in the course of history, the sociological implications, the artistic vision, the impassioned music, the global implications. It was as magnificent as it was awe-inspiring.

Why? Because teachers made us caring, intelligent, thoughtful and insightful people. Teachers helped us realize our potential, our worth, our dreams. Teachers led us on the path to understand true excellence, pride in our work, and an understanding of our universe. Teachers taught us as much about who we wanted to be as who we were.

And as every great thinker in history has known, what we teach is so very much more than any subject; we teach excellence in everything through education. Our purpose is to help young people find happiness in their lives, to experience heights of emotion and thrills of success. To understand that through excellence in doing anything comes the reward of its virtues. To that end, we need to continue to teach, and to expose our students to every facet of learning. We must strive for ever greater heights for our students and for ourselves. In that way we will grow, and our students will grow. We must be our students' guide, the pacesetter, the standard bearer for excellence. Not just for their *education in any one subject*, but for their *education in living*.

When thinking of that aspiration, I often remember a quote that was handed to me on a piece of paper at the end of a session I gave years ago: "Excellence is the result of caring more than others think is wise; risking more than others think is safe. Dreaming more than others think is practical, and expecting more than others think is possible." We touch our students' lives deeply. We touch their lives immeasurably. We help them enjoy living, not just existing. We help them to appreciate the importance of every discipline, the beautiful, the intriguing, the historical, the logical and all other manner of life. Every teacher is like a lighthouse. We don't just offer a light for some to see by, but a torch, a resplendent torch. It may be invisible to some, but it is a beacon for all to follow. We must simply help everyone follow that light.

Yes, some subjects help inform, enlighten and explain. Others develop skills, facility and abilities. Others enhance the power to analyze, synthesize and recognize. While still others foster creativity, fluency, expression and exploration. Why is each necessary? Why is each essential? Renowned film director Federico Fellini may well have given us the key to that question when he stated, "A different language is a different vision of life." For every subject a student learns allows him or her to view the world with a different lens. Whether it's a problem to be solved, a sight to be seen, a sound to be heard, a formula to improve, an event to understand, a conversation to grasp or a discovery to envision, possessing each of those lenses can make all the difference in the world.

Why can't we put it into words? Why can't we describe the capacity of educational excellence? Why can't we really explain to everyone why education is so important to life? Borrowing a sentiment from the great Carlyle: Who is there that in logical words can express the effect education has on us? It leads us to the edge of the infinite, and lets us for moments gaze into it.

Billy knew. All these years later, he is often on my mind, always in my heart and forever in my soul. See—I couldn't tell you. ▨

Epilogue: Passion, Purpose and Promise

Pablo Picasso once affirmed, "Everything you can imagine is real." Who more than a teacher can understand the truth of that simple statement or the responsibility in its message? For we have dedicated ourselves to *imagining* what our students can become and to helping them make it real. Day by day, challenge by challenge, step by step, we help each of them accomplish what started in the imagination as a hope, a wish, a dream.

Let us never lose sight of that goal. Let us never stop seeing what isn't there, seeing what our students can become. Let us never forget those amazing, extraordinary words of Henry David Thoreau: "The question is not what you look at, but what you see."

Each of us chose teaching—or maybe teaching chose us. We are teachers; it is what we do and who we are. It is our passion. It is our purpose. It is our promise. Our life's work begins with paper, pens, books and rulers. It ends with lives that are changed forever. What we teach is as much about what is learned as how it is learned, what can be expressed in words as much as about what *cannot* be expressed in words. We help young people to see what is visible as much as what is invisible, and to know as much about what can be understood as about what can't be understood. We help them to develop their skills as much as their minds, their hearts as much as their souls. We are teachers; it's just what we do. For those who have dedicated their lives to this calling, no explanation is necessary. For those who have not, no explanation can suffice. Maybe Blaise Pascal said it best: "The heart has its reasons which reason knows not of."

As teachers we are inextricably linked to our students, our world and humanity. We collectively hold the future of our young people, thus the future of our world, in our hands. Our students' happiness, understanding and experiences are our responsibility. The future truly is ours. We can shape the reality to come. And in that way we live the words of Peter F. Drucker: "The best way to predict the future is to create it." For as Albert Pike stated so eloquently, "What we do for ourselves dies with us. What we do for others remains, and is immortal." Each of you shares your talents, skills, knowledge, love and compassion with your students. Each of you shares yourself, your heart and soul. And that gift will live on for generation after generation to come and touch the lives of those whom you will never know.

In an earlier chapter, I talked about listening to a speech by the remarkable educator and entertainer Shari Lewis. As I listened to each passing word, I became ever more electrified by her thoughts. And I can think of no better way to close this book than to share the simple power of a phrase she spoke that day. Calmly, almost solemnly, she said, "As teachers, you will teach as much with who you are as with what you know." That is why we are teachers. We treasure learning, cherish our students, reveal our hearts, embrace humanity, and touch the soul of eternity. Our passion for education is only equaled by our passion to help those who wish to learn its wonders.

May the passion of what brought you to your subject empower you. May the purpose of what brought you to teaching swell your heart. May the promise of what brought you into the lives of all those whom you teach fill you with wonder, joy and happiness. May the passion you have for teaching ever strengthen your purpose. May your dedication to your students be matched only by the joy they bring you. May you spend all the days of your life cherishing the wonder that is you, and the profound impact you have on all those whom you teach. Walk with them, excite them, empower them, make them curious, push them, and gently invite them to grow. For that is your promise, it is your passion, it is your calling, it is your mission, it is your purpose.

ABOUT THE AUTHOR

Called "one of the most exciting and exhilarating voices in music education today," Dr. Peter Loel Boonshaft has been invited to speak or conduct in every state in the nation and around the world. He is the author of three critically acclaimed best selling books and numerous articles for educational journals and magazines. Currently a Professor of Music at Hofstra University, he lives on Long Island, New York with his wife and three children. ▨